Introduction

For over 14 years the *Canberra* and the *Sea Princess* together have represented P&O Cruises, and even though they were designed for very different purposes, the two ships do have a lot in common. They were both products of UK shipyards in the 1960s, at a time of very rapid decline in this once major industry. They both came from shipbuilders with a reputation for the very best work, who, sadly, incurred huge financial losses as a result of these contracts. Happily the two vessels have weathered the painful transition from passenger liner to cruise ship, necessitated by changing trends in the 1970s. It is also worth recording that they are two of only a handful of passenger ships which were built in UK shipyards and which remain, over two decades later, under the Red Ensign, although the *Sea Princess* started her career under a foreign flag.

Today they spend the greater part of the year cruising from Southampton, and in the winter months they cruise around the world, usually circumnavigating the globe in opposite directions. Holiday-makers are offered a uniquely British atmosphere on board, which would still be recognized by travellers who knew P&O in the late 1930s, with curry luncheons and afternoon teas. However, they also offer the comforts of the modern, purpose-built cruise ships, with the same 'Broadway' style entertainments and the spectacular shipboard 'theme' nights.

No one can be certain how much longer these two ships will grace the oceans of the world, but at the Meyer Werft shipyard in Papenburg, Germany, work is now under way on P&O's new 67,000 gross ton cruise liner, which will be named *Oriana*.

I hope that this book will serve as more than just a souvenir of two cruise liners, and that it will be a tribute to two magnificent British ships, which are admired the world over.

Neil McCart
September 1993

To Freda

Jacket Design Freda McCart

© Neil McCart/FAN PUBLICATIONS 1993

Front Cover: Canberra arrives in Southampton on 26 June 1976 from a Mediterranean cruise/*Sea Princess* at Southampton in the early 1980s.   (*Don Smith*)

Inside Front Cover: The *Canberra* at Southampton ready for service once again after her post-Falklands refurbishment.
(*N. McCart*)

Inside Back Cover: The *Sea Princess* in dry dock at Southampton.
(*P&O*)

ISBN 0-9519538-2-6

Typesetting and Printing by
D. W. Jones (Printers) Ltd.,
Beverley Street,
Port Talbot,
West Glamorgan,
SA13 1DY

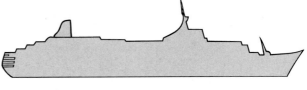

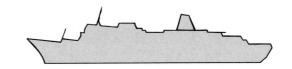

Contents

Published by FAN PUBLICATIONS
17 Wymans Lane Cheltenham GL51 9QA England
0242 580290

Chapter One

Canberra - A Ship For The Future

Canberra's superstructure takes shape whilst the hull is still on the stocks. Here the Crow's Nest and the Stadium can be seen under construction.   *(P&O)*

In the immediate post-war years thousands of people wanted to emigrate to Australia from the United Kingdom, and in those days there was only one way to travel such a long distance - by passenger liner. Most of the new Australians travelled under the Assisted Passage Scheme, becoming what were popularly known as 'Ten Pound Tourists'. There were many reasons for this mass emigration, not least among them being the austere post-war conditions in Britain, and Australia's desperate need to populate its vast territory. During the Second World War, at the peak of their offensive in 1942, the Japanese bombed Darwin and almost reached Port Moresby at the south-eastern tip of New Guinea. With the fall of Singapore, it became painfully apparent that Australia could no longer rely on the Royal Navy, or the 'mother country' for its defence against external aggression. It was against this background that the Australian government encouraged European immigration in an effort to increase the population and develop a sense of national security.

Unlike today, when modern travellers can jet to Australia in about 24 hours, the 'Ten Pound' migrants of the 1940s and 1950s were setting off on a long sea voyage to a far distant land. There was little prospect of them ever seeing the land of their birth or many of their loved ones again. The decorative streamers, which make today's cruise departure so exciting, had a much deeper and more poignant significance for those on board and their friends and relatives on the quayside.

It was 1949 before the last of the company's passenger liners was released from government service following the end of the Second World War, and this coincided with the *Himalaya's* maiden voyage. In the early 1950s the *Arcadia* and *Iberia* entered the Australian service. All these post-war vessels were improvements on the pre-war *Straths,* but in the

Canberra's huge hull dominates Harland and Wolff's shipyard in early 1960 as she lies on the stocks only a few weeks before launching. In the background is the Royal Mail Lines vessel *Aragon*   *(Author's Collection)*

Arcadia and Iberia greater emphasis was placed on the tourist class accommodation to cater for the assisted passage migrants. By 1955 the P&O Company had to consider replacements for the first two 'white sisters' of the 1930s, the *Strathnaver* and *Strathaird*. These two 22,000 tonners had made their maiden voyages in late 1931 and early 1932 respectively, and during the Second World War they had been requisitioned as troop transports, during which time they had been steamed hard for long periods, with only the minimum of maintenance. However, there was another, more important, reason for considering replacing them and that was the prospect of a profitable trade which could be won in the Pacific Ocean.

Dame Pattie Menzies releases the launching switch and sends a bottle of Australian wine, decorated with a sprig of heather, onto the *Canberra's* bulbous bow. *(P&O)*

The employees of Harland & Wolff turn out on an overcast, damp day, to watch as the *Canberra* enters the water for the first time. *(Harland & Wolff)*

The Orient Line, which was part of the P&O Group, was extending its voyages to Australia into the Pacific Ocean, and it was decided that a new joint P&O and Orient Line fleet could provide three new routes which would cover this vast area. The first would extend traditional line voyages from Sydney to New Zealand and the West Coast of North America. The second route linked Hong Kong and Japan with North America, while the third route provided a triangular service between Australia, Asia and the USA. These new itineraries meant longer voyages and in order to shorten the sailing time, greater speeds would be necessary. The technical requirements for the new service demanded larger and faster ships than the *Arcadia* and *Iberia,* but at the same time vessels which could use P&O's traditional route to Australia, via the Mediterranean, Suez, Aden and Colombo.

In 1956 P&O sought tenders from major shipbuilding companies for a new vessel, and on 20 December they informed Harland & Wolff of Belfast that they were placing the order with them. A month later details of the specifications required were given to the Press. The new liner was to be of 45,000 gross tons, the largest ship ever built for the company, with an overall length of 814ft and a beam of 103 ft, and a range of 10,000 miles without refuelling. Several innovative features were incorporated into her design, including placing the propulsion machinery aft, which in those days was unusual in a ship of that size. She was to be fitted with turbo-electric machinery and have a welded aluminium superstructure. The passenger accommodation would cater for 1,650 in the tourist class, more than in any of the company's previous ships, and 600 first class passengers. The interior decoration was to be directed by Sir Hugh Casson in association with Messrs McInnes, Gardner & Partners.

On 23 January 1957 the order, worth £15 million to Harland & Wolff, was officially confirmed. Eight months of detailed design and preparation work followed before the first keel plates of yard number 1621 were laid on 23 September at slipway 14, Queen's Island, Belfast. Over the next few years, as work progressed, there was a great deal of publicity for the new liner as a builder's model of this, 'ship that shapes the future', was displayed at a number of national and international exhibitions. As always, one of the main areas of speculation was the vessel's name, and in March 1958 Sir Donald Anderson, who was attending a dinner with Australia's leading political press correspondents in Canberra, announced that, 'The ship will be called the *Canberra.'* Sir Donald went on, 'In building this new ship the P&O Company is assuming the continuance of British migration to Australia and the need for passenger ships to carry them in the most up-to-date conditions. A continuance of an active migration programme is necessary for the company to justify the investment of £15 million in this ship. We estimate that a ship of this size and cost cannot be made to operate at a profit on the UK-Australia trade alone, but we look to obtaining adequate earnings by extending voyages across the Pacific.' The name was, in the event, an inspired choice as far as public relations were concerned, because P&O, in common with other British fleets operating in the antipodes, had received a good deal of criticism from 'nationalist' politicians. By naming their future flagship after Australia's capital, the P&O Company symbolized the common interest between Britain and Australia.

Sadly, during the late 1950s, the shipbuilding industry was bedevilled by industrial troubles and in April 1959, after a strike by platers at Harland & Wolff, it was apparent that the *Canberra's* completion schedule had slipped back somewhat. It was Wednesday 16 March 1960, some four months later than had been planned, when she eventually took to the water. It was a day of great celebration in Belfast, for the *Canberra* was the biggest ship launched there since the completion of the White Star liner *Britannic* 46 years previously, in 1914. The day began with overcast skies and rain but, for the launch itself at noon, the weather cleared and Dame Pattie Menzies, the wife of the Australian Prime Minister, released the launching switch and sent the huge white hull thundering down the slipway. At a luncheon afterwards the P&O chairman, Sir William Currie, spoke of his company's determination, 'to endeavour to keep British shipping supreme.' Dame Pattie Menzies declared that the *Canberra* would be, 'like a hand of friendship stretching across the sea' for everyone who travelled in her.

It was over a year after the launching ceremony, and still over three months behind schedule, before the *Canberra* was ready to undergo her builder's trials, which were conducted in Belfast Lough on 29 April 1961. While she was steaming at speed one major problem became apparent, in that the bows of the ship lifted almost clear of the water. Two days later she was in Southampton's King George V dry dock, where this unforeseen problem was resolved by pumping hundreds of tons of cement into her forward compartments. She spent over two weeks in the port, during which time she was visited by HRH the Duke of Edinburgh, and work continued to complete the fitting out. She left Southampton for the Clyde and her acceptance trials, with 400 company guests on board, at just after 9pm on 16 May 1961. Once again she was behind schedule, but this time the delay was due to a small fire in the lagging of some engine-room piping.

After a fast overnight passage north, the *Canberra* ran her speed trials off the Isle of Arran, and over the measured mile she reached a speed of 29.27 knots.

After successfully completing her trials, and having been formally handed over to P&O, the new liner left the Tail of the Bank at 10.38pm on Saturday 20 May 1961. During the voyage south she kept close inshore so that holiday-makers at seaside resorts along the west and south coasts had a chance to see Britain's newest and biggest passenger liner to be built since the end of the Second World War.

During the two-day voyage from the Clyde to Dover, and then back to Southampton, watchers on shore had no difficulty in recognizing the distinctive feature of twin buff funnels, set side by side and well aft. On board, as well as 600 journalists and travel agents, 300 workmen from Harland & Wolff worked round the clock to complete the fitting out of the public rooms, work which was still continuing in the early morning of Tuesday 23 May 1961, when the *Canberra* tied up alongside 106 berth in Southampton Docks.

Having shown off this lovely new liner to the country, preparations had to be made for her maiden voyage.

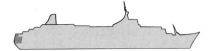

Chapter Two

Shipshape Design For Shipboard Life

Canberra's spacious Sun Deck, sheltered from the elements by wind-breaks on both sides and by the terraced superstructure forward, provides an excellent recreational area for passengers.
(P&O)

'Shipshape is an adjective of praise which even the most determined landlubber understands,' declared Sir Hugh Casson in respect of his design of the *Canberra's* passenger accommodation. 'It describes a visual quality - a sense of fitness for purpose combined with instinctive grace, that makes every ship, large or small, something more than an assembly of bits and pieces.' In March 1957 the design team set out to produce an interior which would appear as cosy in Southampton Docks on a cold, grey day in February, as it would in the sweltering heat of the Red Sea. Sir Hugh also recognized that the new ship would have a long life and while it was impossible to ignore fashion, he felt that it was important not to become its prisoner. With the *Canberra* he wanted simple forms, clean surfaces and clear colours and whilst sprinklers and air-conditioning ducts were necessary, he did not want them pressed onto the passengers' attention. Today, just over 32 years after she carried her first passen-

gers, the *Canberra* remains an individual ship with her own distinct 'personality' and Sir Hugh Casson has every reason to be proud of his unique design, where passengers can still meet, eat and play in imaginative settings.

Although the Shaw Savill liner *Southern Cross* had pioneered the idea of a 'one-class' ship, with facilities open to all the passengers, this was very much an exception to the rule on British liners and in this aspect the *Canberra* conformed to the first and tourist class configuration, as had all P&O liners since 1931. As before, the first class section was amidships and the public rooms included a lounge and adjoining cocktail bar (Meridian Room and Century Bar), a private room for dining or entertaining (Crystal Room), an observation lounge (Crow's Nest), a ballroom (Bonito Club) and a dining-room (Pacific Restaurant).

The Meridian Room, which is at the forward end of the Promenade Deck, has an open-plan design and, by means of

The Meridian Room, at the forward end of the Promenade Deck has an open-plan design. This view, taken in 1961, shows the original spiky and angular 30ft-long ceiling light which was made up of glittering metal facets. *(P&O)*

A spiral staircase rises up from the Meridian Room on the Promenade Deck, to the Crow's Nest Bar. When this view was taken in 1961 it was the first class observation lounge. Today it boasts a central bar and a grand piano. *(P&O)*

a series of curving bulkheads, other small compartments are formed within the 'folds'. Within another 'fold' the staircase rises up as a brightly-lit white spiral to the Crow's Nest. At the forward end the curving walls enclose the 'sit-up' Century Bar, the counter for which has been designed as a sculptural shape formed by laminations of dark-coloured hardwoods. Acting as a foil to the curving screen walls, the main central seating area of the lounge was originally illuminated by a spiky and angular 30ft-long ceiling light fitting, which was made up of glittering metal facets. The overall effect in the room was, and still is, obtained from the style of the chairs which were originally a special glass fibre 'shell-like' design, a welcome departure from the tradition of 'club' armchairs in ships' lounges.

are inset flush with the ceiling panels. The two bar and pantry service areas are concealed by large rectangular screens which originally displayed illuminated feature maps in relief of Southampton Water and Sydney Harbour. Other interesting features of the room, which are still in place, are the scale model navigation buoys. The original furniture was of the celebrated 'Bertoia' design, with chairs constructed of chromium plate and wire basket and upholstered in yellow and white tweeds. Today, apart from the furnishings, the Crow's Nest does not look too different from its appearance over 30 years ago.

Today the Meridian Room provides a comfortable lounge for concerts and quiet relaxation. *(P&O)*

The first class Games Deck was originally situated aft of the Crow's Nest Bar and it featured a sliding deckhead which could be closed in inclement weather. This can be seen in the photograph. This area is now the Stadium Theatre, with the stage directly beneath what used to be the sliding deckhead. *(P&O)*

The spiral staircase from the Meridian Room led up to the centre of the Crow's Nest observation lounge or, as it is known today, the Crow's Nest Piano Bar. The design of this room emphasizes the sweeping curves of the forward bulkhead which has 41 full-height windows which give a magnificent view forward over the ship's bow. Originally similar windows aft looked out onto the enclosed Games Deck, which is now the Stadium, the focal point for passenger entertainment. All the wall surfaces of the Crow's Nest are flush and painted in an eggshell white with concealed lighting. Main lighting is from clusters of small spotlights which

Aft of the Crow's Nest and the forward staircase is the Bonito Club which was the first class ballroom. The after bulkhead was designed to slide vertically into the floor so that dancing and entertainment can continue out onto the terraced pool area. The tables at each side of the dance floor are illuminated internally, and the teak barrier which was at the sides of the dance floor has given way to a stainless steel handrail.

The Crystal Room, on the starboard side of the Promenade Deck, is one room which still remains the same as it was in

1961, with its bulkheads of light grey wood veneer in parquet strips. The first class children's playroom was on the starboard side of the Games Deck and was decorated in pale blue. On the walls there were murals of children at play and famous characters from children's books. One half of the room could be opened up in fine weather to give access to an outside deck space.

The Stadium Theatre, completely unrecognizable as the former Games Deck. *(N. McCart)*

The first class Pacific Restaurant is on E Deck, extending over the full 100 feet of the ship's width, forward of the galley and food preparation areas. Today it caters for passengers in forward cabins. The primary aims in designing this compartment were to minimize the impact of a very large area and offset any feeling of oppression which the lack of natural daylight might give. The first problem was solved by raising a section of the deckhead and designing a sunken

area in the centre of the room, with steps down into it, which softened the visual effect. The use of pillar-casings to form screen walls means that the whole room is not visible from any one point, and further visual dividers are high-backed banquette seats in bays on either side of the ship. Each bay seats 12 and is, in effect, a small room on its own.

The tourist class public rooms included a lounge (William Fawcett Room), a bar (Cricketers' Tavern), a smoking room (Peacock Room), a pool café (Alice Springs Room), a ballroom (Island Room) and a teenagers' room (Pop Inn).

The Ocean Room on the Promenade Deck. Originally this room was the tourist class lounge, the William Fawcett Room. Its very size removes any feeling of intimacy. *(N. McCart)*

The main tourist class lounge, on the Promenade Deck, was the William Fawcett Room, which was designed along the lines of the 'Palm Court' with fountains and a considerable amount of mirror glass. In the centre of the room there were two fountains through which bubbling fluorescent

The Peacock Room at the after end of the Promenade Deck was designed as the tourist class smoking room. Today it is called Neptune's and it fulfils the role of a night-club. *(N. McCart)*

The tourist class ballroom on the Games Deck was the Island Room. This view, taken in 1961 looking from starboard to port, shows the furniture laid out in 'islands' on white rugs. *(P&O)*

The long, narrow room is divided down its length by individual tables with semi-circular seats, and, as the name suggests, cricket is the theme here. The inboard bulkhead, which is veneered with willow strips, is a montage of cricket bats, balls, caps, pads, gloves and stumps. Fixed at right angles to the outboard bulkhead are screens on which life-sized portraits of famous cricketers are painted. The room is truly a cricket lover's paradise, and it has changed little in more than 30 years.

The Peacock Room at the after end of the Promenade Deck, now known as Neptune's, was originally designed as the tourist class smoking room for 'smoking and reading'. At its after end there were two adjoining rooms in which passengers could enjoy a game of cards. The floor was white and the central dance floor was marked with diagonal black stripes. The curved bulkheads were covered with a dyed blue wood veneer and the curtains, with their attractive peacock designs, formed a continuous wall-covering when drawn. Today the room fulfils the role of a night-club rather than just a smoking room.

The tourist class ballroom on the Games Deck was the Island Room, and over the years it has undergone so many changes that it is virtually unrecognizable now. In the early years the port side was also used as a playground for the children, but this space is now occupied by a self-service buffet. The laminated plywood furniture was laid out in 'islands' on white rugs, whereas today, white plastic tables and chairs cater for passengers using the buffet. On the star-

water spiralled upwards and then captured small ornamental balls. However, this idea was found to be most impractical and the fountains were removed after the ship's trials. Today the Ocean Room is still very much a central meeting point in the ship, but its very size removes any feeling of intimacy. The main tourist class bar was the Cricketers' Tavern, which today still incorporates the atmosphere of an English 'pub'.

The tourist class restaurant, the Atlantic Restaurant, was the largest dining-room afloat in the early 1960s, with seating for 704 people. *(P&O)*

The recent addition of teak-veneered dividers with coloured glass panels has helped to give the Atlantic Restaurant a more 'exclusive' atmosphere. *(N.McCart)*

board side there is a bar which was added in 1982. Outside the Island Room the two large open and exposed areas of deck have been screened off from the elements to provide further seating at buffet mealtimes.

The starboard side of the Island Room, looking aft and showing the bar area which was added in 1982. *(P&O Cruises)*

The Alice Springs Café and lido area remains very much as it was in 1961. The lounge opens out onto a swimming-pool and cane furniture is still a feature of the room. When the *Canberra* was built, her tourist class dining saloon, the Atlantic Restaurant, was the largest dining-room afloat, with seating accommodation for 704 people. Along both outboard sides of the room the seating is divided into bays to dispel a 'canteen' appearance and this has been achieved without spoiling the vista across the vast compartment. The fairly recent additions of teak-veneered dividers with coloured glass sections has helped to give the Atlantic Restaurant a more 'exclusive' atmosphere.

A large cinema, capable of seating 332 people, is situated centrally on A Deck, and was available to both first and tourist class passengers. The tourist class playroom, which is now the Junior Club on the port side of the Games Deck, was decorated with murals of imaginary birds and animals

along both ends of the room and in a semi-circle behind the carousel. There was a large Wendy House, a traditional wooden rocking-horse and a variety of wooden prams and trolleys. Many former passengers will remember this room with affection and today, although its position has been changed, the playhouse is still there. So too are the rocking-horse and the wooden toys, to be enjoyed by holiday-makers now, rather than 'ten pound' migrants.

The Games Deck on the starboard side aft, looking forward towards the Island Room. This area, on both port and starboard sides, was originally part of the tourist class section and screens have now been installed to shelter passengers wishing to use the Island Room buffet. *(N. McCart)*

A large proportion of the first class staterooms were arranged in groups looking out onto courts with three large windows in the ship's side, although for those who wanted even more space and luxury there were four verandah suites and eight de luxe cabins. In the tourist class section there were single, two-and four-berth cabins and some of the latter could be converted into two-berth rooms with a shower and wc. Nowadays, with *Canberra* operating as a one-class ship, it is this wide variety of accommodation which adds to the vessel's popularity. Generally, the *Canberra* is an easy ship to find one's way around, but some passengers will find the experiences of a senior P&O official who toured the new ship in 1961 very familiar: 'I had been prepared for something out of the ordinary when I had my first look at the new ship, but I must confess to having been impressed far beyond my expectations. Once aboard I became bewildered, for *Canberra* did not conform to the usual layout of P&O ships and it took 15 minutes to find my cabin. With the engines further aft, the great central section of the ship is given over to cabins; gone are the long, white painted alley-ways, and corridors have a habit of turning off at right angles. The most remarkable view is from the bridge, when looking aft, one sees an amazing expanse of sundecks below, both first and tourist, with glass screens along the sides. Let us give the travelling public what they want. Let us make sea travel popular and capture a generation. This magnificent new ship will do just that.'

P&O's proposed new service into the Pacific Ocean demanded not only a much larger ship, but also, in order to reduce the voyage time to Australia, a considerably more powerful vessel than any which the company had built previously. Before deciding on the type of machinery which would be most suitable for a ship such as the *Canberra*, extensive design studies were undertaken, on behalf of P&O, by the Yarrow-Admiralty Research Department. It was decided to adopt a turbo-electric system driving twin propellers and capable of developing 85,000SHP. In 1961 this gave the *Canberra* the most powerful British-built turbo-electric

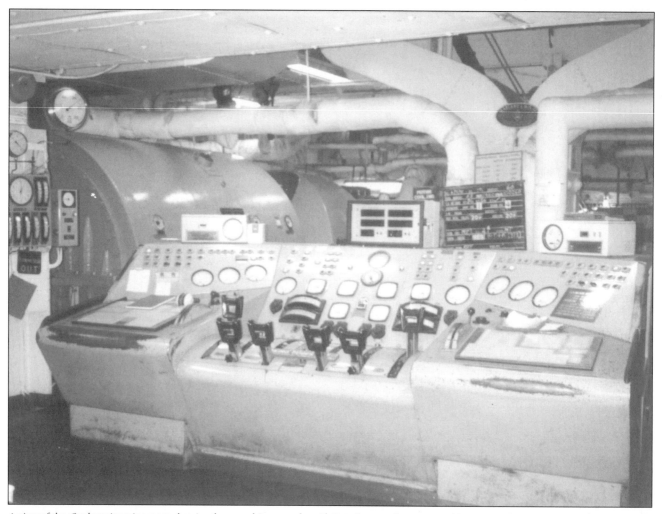

A view of the *Canberra's* engine-room showing the propulsion console, with its twin-screw lever gear and instrumentation. *(N. W. Pound)*

propulsion installation and her power per shaft - 42,500SHP - exceeded that of the French pre-war liner *Normandie*. This method of propulsion had first been used by P&O in 1928 in their luxurious, but ill-fated, passenger liner *Viceroy of India*.

There were a number of advantages in choosing this type of machinery and placing it right aft in the ship. Not only did it allow for improved passenger accommodation, but it also provided a much greater flexibility in the arrangement. The boilers could be arranged above and aft of the propeller motors, allowing for short runs of steam piping to the turbo-alternators which are forward of the propulsion motors. Three Foster Wheeler external superheater D-type (ESD) boilers supply steam at 750psi and at a temperature of 960°F to the two British Thomson-Houston (BT-H) turbo-alternators, and these in turn provide the power for two 42-pole synchronous propeller motors. As well as the flexibility already referred to, for economical cruising, both the propeller motors can be powered by one turbo-alternator.

Safety was also uppermost in the designers' minds, and the ship originally carried 24 lifeboats which could accommodate 3,362 people. There were six, 36-ft motor boats and two smaller motor boats specifically designed as 'accident boats', fitted with radio equipment, while the remaining boats were fitted with hand propelling gear. Two of these boats have since been replaced by pontoons for use when the ship has to anchor offshore. However, unlike previous ships which stowed their lifeboats high up on the Boat Deck, the

Canberra's boats are tucked away above the Promenade Deck. In every respect the *Canberra* was indeed, 'ship-shape'.

One of the *Canberra's* main turbo-alternators, which bears the British Thomson-Houston Company's maker's plate. Although the design and production of the *Canberra's* electrical machinery was started by BT-H, the company was taken over by Associated Electrical Industries Ltd., and so it has always been described as being of AEI manufacture.

(N. W. Pound)

Chapter Three

The Old Enemy - Distance

The *Canberra* in Southampton Water on 1 May 1961. This aerial view shows off her spacious open decks to their best advantage.   *(FotoFlite)*

In 1788 Australia's first fleet of 11 small vessels, with a combined tonnage which was less than one-tenth that of the *Canberra*, set sail for Botany Bay. After a voyage of 231 days and 15,063 miles by way of Rio and the Cape of Good Hope, they anchored at their destination. In the years that followed, shorter routes and better ships narrowed this immense gulf between the European and Australian continents. In 1896 the opening of the Suez Canal reduced the distance considerably, but even as late as the 1920s P&O liners still took 46 days to reach Sydney from

The *Canberra* in the English Channel, May 1961.   *(FotoFlite)*

Tilbury. In 1931 the *Strathnaver* cut the voyage time by six days and in the mid-1950s the *Arcadia* and *Iberia* made the voyage in 35 days, but this was still well over four weeks at sea. However, with the *Canberra's* service speed of 22 knots the passage between Southampton, which was to be *Canberra's* home port, and Sydney could be completed in 25 days. With no real competition from the airline companies, this was a major advance in world travel and it brought Australia that much 'closer' to Europe.

So, at 4pm on Friday 2 June 1961, with the good wishes of the millions who had seen and read about her over the preceding four years, the *Canberra* left Southampton's 106 berth, commanded by Commodore G. A. Wild, for her maiden voyage to Sydney and the Pacific. It was a good omen for the vessel's future and a testimony to her potential drawing power, that on what was an out-of-season voyage, she was fully booked with 2,238 passengers. Some were making the short voyage to Gibraltar and Naples, but most were going all the way to Australia and amongst these were 750 emigrants setting out for a new life in the antipodes.

As well as being the *Canberra's* first commercial voyage, P&O did all they could to make it a goodwill trip to demonstrate to as many people as possible this product of British skill and artistry. After leaving Naples at 6pm on 6 June 1961, the *Canberra* set course for the Suez Canal and made her southbound transit three days later. She arrived in Aden early on the morning of Monday 12 June, but while at the port she suffered a complete loss of electrical power, which was caused by leaking tubes in the port condenser, a problem which had first become apparent earlier in the voyage. This

Dressed overall, the *Canberra* is alongside Southampton's 106 berth shortly before leaving on her maiden voyage.

(Maritime Photo Library)

resulted in an uncomfortable 14-hour delay and *Canberra* did not leave Aden until 2pm on 13 June.

The first great welcome of the voyage was at Fremantle and although she was, by that time, 31 hours behind schedule, the shore was lined with cheering crowds. Unfortunately her departure was delayed for an hour because of mechanical problems, and it was just before 11pm on 23 June before she left for Melbourne. While she was steaming across the Australian Bight, 10 miles from the coast, the condenser trouble recurred and speed had to be reduced again. Although she was almost a day late in reaching Melbourne, thousands of people crowded the port quays, the approaches and the

On 29 June 1961 the *Canberra* arrives alongside the Overseas Passenger Terminal, Circular Quay, Sydney for the first time.

(P&O)

Flying the 'Stars & Stripes' at her mast-head, the *Canberra* receives a spectacular welcome in San Francisco on 20 July 1961. *(P&O)*

Port Phillip beaches to witness the arrival of the great liner during the morning of 27 June. One of those in the crowd was Dame Pattie Menzies, who had come especially to see 'her' ship arrive and she embarked for the 26½-hour voyage round the coast to Sydney.

The *Canberra* arrived off Sydney Heads during the early afternoon of Thursday 29 June 1961 and once again crowds of people waved from the foreshores. Many small craft met the liner near Sydney Heads and followed her up the harbour, perhaps none more original than a student paddling along in an upturned umbrella.

During her four-day stop-over in the port the ship's engineers worked hard to cure the leaking port condenser and she sailed again at 7pm on 3 July for New Zealand and the Pacific Ocean. Both Auckland and Honolulu greeted the *Canberra* in their own traditional manner, although the visit to the former port was marred by thick fog. The call at Vancouver on 17 July was quite spectacular with hundreds of small boats surrounding the liner and the city bedecked with 'Welcome *Canberra*' banners. When she left the port during the evening of Tuesday 18 July 1961 she was carrying her first stowaway, a 26-year-old Australian, who was found hiding in a life-jacket locker by a Bell Boy only five hours before the ship docked at San Francisco. The *Canberra* cleared the Golden Gate Bridge just before midday and large crowds welcomed her to Pier 32 for a two-day stay in the port. Yet another spectacular welcome awaited the ship in Long Beach, from where she steamed back across the Pacific Ocean to Honolulu and, once again, New Zealand. This time she visited Wellington where she encountered storms, which meant she had to steam outside the harbour for two days in winds of up to Force 12, before she could enter the port which had been closed. However, Commodore Wild remarked that during this severe weather, '... the ship behaved like a lady, and caused very little discomfort.'

The *Canberra* arrived back in Sydney on 10 August 1961,

and on the following day she left for Southampton via the Australian ports then Colombo, Aden, Suez, Naples and Gibraltar, arriving back at her home port during the morning of 4 September. Later that same month she left for Sydney once more and the US West Coast, but again the voyage was marred by machinery problems which, more than once, caused her to fall behind schedule and she did not return to Southampton until 18 December. After undergoing an overhaul of the machinery, she began her third voyage from Southampton on 2 January 1962, steaming out to Sydney via Suez and arriving on 29 January, after a voyage of some 27 days. After visiting the West Coast of North America she again returned via Suez and docked in Southampton on 29 March 1962, the whole voyage having taken less than three months.

The start of *Canberra's* fourth voyage east was delayed by 24 hours in order that maintenance work on the boilers could be completed, and she left Southampton on 19 April 1962. However, yet again she was dogged by machinery problems which not only caused delays, but also excessive fuel consumption. As a result it was decided to cut the voyage short so that she could be given an extended overhaul by Vosper Thorneycroft at Southampton. Making the remainder of the journey at reduced speed, she left Sydney on 20 May and after calling at Auckland, Honolulu and Los Angeles, she made her first transit of the Panama Canal on 11 June 1962 and was, at that time, the widest commercial vessel to have passed through the waterway. She then made a call at Curacao and an unscheduled stop at Trinidad on 14 June, before arriving in Southampton on 21 June 1962, when she went straight into dry dock.

As well as giving her main propulsion machinery a thorough overhaul, 5ft-long extensions were fitted to the funnels to help prevent large soot marks discolouring them. Another significant alteration which was carried out was on the first class stadium at the forward end of the Games Deck, aft of the Crow's Nest Bar. This area, which had been intended to provide the first class passengers with a sheltered area for deck games, had been fitted with a sliding deckhead so that it could be completely enclosed in inclement weather, but it had not been a great success and the compartment was permanently covered and converted into a theatre.

Following her refit, the *Canberra* returned to service on 20 July 1962 with a 12-day cruise to Madeira and Gibraltar, after which she made two transatlantic cruises to New York and back. These cruises had been highly publicized and there was some speculation that both the *Canberra* and *Oriana* would operate regular summer services on the Atlantic. With minimum return fares in the first class set at £162 and in the tourist class at £72, this would have provided tough competition for Cunard, but the *Canberra* was not built for the North Atlantic and such ideas were never seriously considered. However, the 3,500 British tourists on these cruises received the stirring New York welcome from fireboat hoses, ships' sirens and tugboat whistles, together with myriads of small boats. Despite the Atlantic fog and mist the two cruises were a great success and these were followed by a sojourn in the Mediterranean, which of course is more in the tradition of 'sunshine' cruising.

After returning to Southampton on 9 September 1962, the *Canberra* returned to her usual itinerary to Sydney and on into the Pacific Ocean. She returned to Southampton in mid-December that year and Commodore Wild, who had commanded her from the beginning, retired and was replaced by Captain L.A. Hill DSC RD RNR, who was also appointed Commodore of the P&O fleet. His first voyage, which started from Southampton on Sunday 30 December 1962, was another journey to Sydney and the US West Coast. It was a bitterly cold day during a particularly severe winter in the UK, and the 2,230 passengers, many of whom were emigrants, must have felt a sense of relief as they left the Solent. The ship called at Naples on Thursday 3 January 1963 after which she was due at Port Said two days later. At midnight on the evening of 3/4 January she passed south through the Straits of Messina and four hours later she was in a position Lat 37° - 18' N/Long 17° - 20'E, about 160 miles from Malta and steaming south-south-east. However, down below on the starboard main switchboard, an engineer noticed that one of the three turbo-generators which was in use had shed its load. He tried to bring it back onto the board but he was unable to do so and because, not only was it 'off load' but 'motoring', another engineer tried to trip a circuit-breaker in order to isolate it, but he too had no success. Believing, mistakenly, that severe damage might result if the machine continued to 'motor', and that there was no other way of dealing with the problem, he manually forced a circuit-breaker in conditions which were not only contrary to recognized practice, but also contrary to a large warning notice which was posted on the spot. The result of this action was an electrical arc of such severity that experts could not understand how the individual concerned was not incinerated. Fortunately neither of the two engineers was seriously hurt, but the resulting fire continued to be fed electrically by the other two generators and caused severe damage to the vessel's switchboard.

The first that the passengers knew of the emergency was a sudden awakening by the ship's alarm bells, and tourist class passengers on the lower decks were engulfed by thick, pungent, black smoke. One passenger in the tourist class recalls: 'The smoke on D Deck was very thick. I could just see crew members dashing by in the smoke. On C Deck we could breathe a little easier and the Promenade Deck was clear. The only lights we had were from the lifeboats' floodlights.'

However, a passenger in the forward section had an entirely different experience: 'Apart from the alarm bells and the fact that the lights were out, there was nothing to indicate what was wrong.' He went on to praise Captain Hill and the, 'resolution in the master's voice when he made the announcement. He asked us calmly to go to boat stations, and to take life-jackets and plenty of warm clothing. Most of the ship was in darkness, but the emergency lighting soon came on and we found our way up top without panic.'

As the passengers made their way to the various public rooms on the Promenade Deck, the fire parties fought the switchboard fire which was extinguished after about an hour. Although some essential services were restored with power from the vessel's emergency generators, the *Canberra* lay helpless without the use of her main propulsion motors as the engineers worked to make temporary repairs. Fortunately help was at hand in the form of the elderly P&O liner *Stratheden*, which was homeward-bound from Australia having left Port Said on 2 January. She stood by about half a mile from the *Canberra* and as many passengers later testified, her presence was a great comfort to them. They would have been even more comforted to know that Royal Navy warships which were in the vicinity, including the cruiser *Lion* and the destroyer *Scorpion*, were also standing by to help the stricken liner.

In the event no assistance was required, for later in the day the *Canberra's* own engineers managed to restore some power to her starboard engine and get the ship under way once again, first of all at four knots, later increasing this to 10 knots. During the night of 4/5 January the *Canberra*, escorted by the *Stratheden*, made her way to Malta and at 9am on 5 January she arrived at Valletta and was moored in Grand Harbour's Bighi Bay. As engineers from Bailey's Dockyard went on board to assess the damage and to arrange for repairs to be made, P&O had to organize alternative transport for over 2,000 passengers.

The Press made a great deal of the complaints which came from a passengers' self-styled 'action committee', but most passengers understood the company's problems. Mr Ford I. Geddes, a P&O director, flew out from London to co-ordinate the massive airlift of passengers to their destinations, and to inspect damage to the ship. He addressed the passengers personally and most of them accepted the offer of a free flight. For those who were on the 'world voyage', P&O laid on passenger ferries from Malta to Naples, from where they flew them home, and the Australian government organized transport on to Australia for the assisted passage emigrants.

By Monday 14 January all but 48 of the *Canberra's* passengers, who refused under any circumstances to leave the ship, had disembarked and at noon that day repairs were completed and a few hours later the *Canberra* left Valletta for Belfast. It had been decided that permanent repairs would be carried out by Harland & Wolff and on 21 January 1963, six days after leaving Valletta, she arrived in Belfast Lough where the remaining passengers disembarked and the ship was taken over once again by her builders.

It was Friday 24 May 1963 before the *Canberra* returned to service, when she sailed to Sydney via Suez and home by the same route. In order to fulfil her summer UK cruising schedule, the usual Pacific voyage was cancelled.

The switchboard fire had highlighted the fact that even in the 1960s the great enemy on the route to Australia was 'the distance', and the fact that aircraft had, at very short notice, transported nearly 2,000 people to Australia within a week, pointed to the threat of competition from air travel, which was to make liners redundant within a very short space of time.

Chapter Four

The New Enemy - Air Travel

A dramatic view of the *Canberra* alongside Sydney's Overseas Passenger Terminal on a warm evening. *(P&O)*

Following the adverse publicity which resulted first from the machinery problems and then from the switchboard fire in the Mediterranean, the *Canberra* settled down to trouble-free service. She made her routine voyages to the antipodes and the Pacific Ocean and she carried out cruise programmes from both Southampton and Sydney. However, although her troubles in the engine-room had been rectified, other factors, not only for the *Canberra* but for all the traditional passenger liners, were beginning to take their toll on trade. First of all the number of emigrants to Australia was falling considerably and P&O had always counted on these passengers to fill up the tourist class berths. Then, in December 1964, the newly formed British Airways took delivery of the Super VC 10 aircraft which could accommodate 163 economy class passengers. The airlines had already shown just what they could do when the *Canberra* was stranded at Malta in January 1963, and business travellers were turning to air travel in ever increasing numbers. Fortunately P&O liners had always undertaken cruising duties and they were ideal vessels for this particular trade, but in the 1960s cruising was not

as popular as it is today.

However, the *Canberra* continued to add new ports of call to her itineraries. Whilst homeward-bound from Sydney via Suez, in March 1964, she became the largest ship ever to call at Alexandria and considerable preparations were required to meet her demands for depth of water and manoeuvring space and, of course, to meet the needs of over 1,600 passengers. That same summer she visited New York again and was berthed at Pier 92. During the course of the 1960s she continued to 'show the flag' world-wide and in March 1966, during a Pacific cruise, she visited the Far East for the first time. On 15 March she called at Yokohama, tying up at the port's South Pier behind the *Cathay*, where she was given a warm welcome. She went on to Kobe and Nagasaki, before visiting Hong Kong for the first time on 22 March, where she tied up alongside the colony's new Ocean Terminal. However, upon her return to Southampton on 12 May she was caught up in one of the most damaging industrial disputes for many years. It was the first strike for 55 years by the National Union of Seamen and it caused serious damage

One of the most damaging industrial disputes of the 1960s was the Seamen's strike of 1966. On Saturday 18 June, in order to provide more quay space, the *Arcadia* was tied up alongside the *Canberra* at Southampton's 102 berth. *(P&O)*

to the merchant service and the national economy alike and, as with all disputes of this kind, it left a legacy of bitterness in the industry. Whether the cause was due to the employers having lost touch with the union representatives or the union executive not reflecting the wishes of its membership is not known, but when the strike appeared to be a certainty, P&O managers received many applications from men who wanted to get to sea before the prescribed date, because any vessel that was at sea or in a foreign port would not be affected by the stoppage. When the strike started on 17 May 1966, the *Canberra* was in Southampton's 106 berth prior to sailing on a four-day Whitsun cruise, followed by a world voyage on 31 May. The former was quickly cancelled and a decision on the latter was deferred as the liner lay idle at 106 berth. On Saturday 18 June, she was moved to 102 berth, behind the Union Castle ships *Edinburgh Castle, Reina del Mar,* and *Good Hope Castle,* which had berthed alongside each other. That same day, in order to provide more quay space, the *Arcadia* was moved from 37 berth and tied up alongside the *Canberra*, while the *Queen Elizabeth* lay at 105/106 berth. For the tourists to Southampton it was a splendid sight, but for the shipping industry it was a sad and damaging dispute.

When the strike ended at midnight on Friday 1 July 1966, five P&O passenger ships and one cargo vessel were laid up in Southampton and London, and the cost to the company proved very substantial. In addition, the interruption of the passenger ships' schedules meant the cancellation of six cruises, with the result that several thousand holiday-makers were disappointed. Other passengers had been kept waiting either in the UK or elsewhere throughout the world whilst the vessels were strike-bound and after the stoppage it was essential to get the ships back on their programmes as soon as possible. A decision had to be made whether to cancel *Canberra's* world voyage, due to start on 31 May, or two Mediterranean cruises in August and September. Had the strike lasted another week or so, the longer voyage would have been abandoned and she would have been kept in Southampton for the cruises. Whatever choice was made, a large number of people were going to be disappointed and the chairman of P&O-Orient Lines, Mr R. M. Thwaites, decided that the *Canberra* must operate her world voyage as thousands of passengers, in various parts of the world, many of them away from their homes, were waiting to travel on the liner. So, at 1pm on Saturday 2 July 1966, she left Southampton for Sydney and the Pacific, sailing by way of Suez.

During this voyage she again broke new ground when, on 9 August, she called at Nuku'alofa, Tonga. The visit had originally been scheduled for February that year, but it had been cancelled because of Queen Salote's death. *Canberra's* arrival was a memorable occasion for all concerned and particularly Captain E. G. H. Riddleshall and Staff Captain D. J. Scott-

Canberra undergoes an overhaul alongside Ocean Terminal in Southampton Docks during the early 1970s.   *(Vosper Thorneycroft)*

Masson, who were invited to the palace where they exchanged greetings with the new King Taufa'ahau Tupou IV.

In June 1967 the outbreak of the Arab-Israeli Six-Day War closed the Suez Canal, which meant that voyages to Australia had to be made via Cape Town or Panama. On the outbreak of war, *Canberra* was in the Eastern Mediterranean, bound for Sydney. Having called at Naples on 4 June, she was due in Port Said at 3.00pm local time two days later, 6 June, the day that war broke out. She received immediate orders to turn round and make for Gibraltar where, after disembarking some of her passengers, she continued the voyage via Las Palmas and Cape Town. Between August 1967 and December 1972 *Canberra* made 11 round voyages to Sydney and the US West Coast. Outward-bound six were made via Cape Town and five via Panama and on the return journey six were made by way of Panama and five by way of Cape Town. These longer routes inevitably meant increased costs, and so, at a time when the demand for berths on line voyages was declining, the *Canberra* began making more cruises. By the early 1970s it was clear that this was the way ahead for the large passenger liners. The wide-bodied Boeing 747 aircraft had suddenly made it possible for hundreds of people to travel to any destination world-wide within 48 hours, and the passenger liners could never compete with this. During 1972 P&O marketed 35 cruises with 47,468 berths to be sold, and although cruise bookings did increase by 8%, it still was not possible to keep all of the ships in service. The first casualties were the *Chusan, Orcades* and *Iberia,* which all went to the Far Eastern shipbreaking yards during the course of 1973, but even after this it was still proving difficult to make the remaining ships pay their way. The *Arcadia* and *Oronsay* were based on the West Coast of North America to cruise as one-class ships and 19 Caribbean

cruises, ranging from 11 to 15 days, all starting and terminating in New York, were planned for the *Canberra*. The class barriers were to be dropped and, in fact, the *Canberra* converted easily into a one-class ship, with most of her public rooms being on the Promenade and Games Decks.

During these uncertain times there were many rumours, including one which linked P&O and Cunard in a merger, with the *Canberra* and *QE2* offering a joint transatlantic and cruising service, but there is no evidence to suggest that this was ever more than just an idea. On 8 January 1973 the *Canberra* docked at Southampton from a Christmas cruise in the Caribbean, amid protests about water rationing which had been imposed on board. She had run short of drinking water because she had been unable to take on sufficient at various ports, and 500 tons which had been promised at St Thomas were not forthcoming. The problem was one for which neither the company nor the ship could be blamed, and it was unwelcome publicity.

During her two-week stay in Southampton the *Canberra* underwent her annual overhaul and the barriers which had separated the first and tourist class sections of the ship were removed. On Wednesday 24 January 1973 she left Southampton for her positioning voyage to New York, and upon her arrival six days later the ship's company had just 36 hours to prepare for the first of P&O's cruises from the USA's East Coast.

The first two cruises were not a success with less than 30% of the accommodation booked, and on 26 February 1973, two days after arriving back in New York from St. Thomas, the *Canberra* was laid up at the mouth of the Cape Fear River, 30 miles from Wilmington, North Carolina. Two cruises which should have taken place during early March were cancelled and the liner's New York cruise programme did not start again until 24 March 1973, when she sailed for Nassau,

The *Canberra* in Southampton's King George V dry dock undergoing an annual refit. Her starboard propeller and tailshaft have both been removed.   *(Vosper Thorneycroft)*

Caracas Bay, Fort de France and St. Thomas. Financially the cruises were a disaster with less than half the accommodation sold on most sailings and on 1 June 1973, at a press conference in London, the P&O Group Executive Director, Mr Richard Adams, announced that the *Canberra* was to be withdrawn from service on 30 September 1973, on completion of her New York cruise programme, and sold. He went on to say: 'Unlike our other passenger ships, in both economic and operational terms, *Canberra* has proved unsuitable for the world-wide cruising role she has had to assume. A feasibility study is at present being carried out to ascertain whether it is technically possible to re-engine the ship to reduce her operating draught from 35ft to about 32ft. Should the exercise prove impracticable or too costly *Canberra* will be sold. In financial terms, if the re-engining exceeds £3 million the ship will be sold. The *Canberra* has a book value of £600,000 although her scrap value now would be in excess of this. P&O will require a substantial premium over scrap value from any purchaser to prevent a conflict of interest.' He went on to say the vessel had been a drain on the company's resources and that she had been losing money for two years. Just over 12 years had passed since her maiden voyage and her career seemed at an end.

A number of former crew members recall that for the remainder of the New York cruise programme the atmosphere on board was tinged with gloom. One cruise which appears to have been an exception, however, began on 23 June 1973, when the ship was chartered by 'Eclipse Cruises Inc'. The passengers were astronomers, including Professor Neil Armstrong of Cincinnati University, better known of course as the first man to set foot on the moon, in 1969. This particular cruise took passengers across the Atlantic to Tenerife, and the highlight of the trip began at 9.15am on Saturday 30 June as the enthusiasts witnessed a total eclipse of the sun. This was, in fact, the second longest such event in history and would not be equalled in duration for another 177 years. Alan Hale, the *Canberra's* Purser, recalls the occasion: 'From the moon's shadow first touching the sun to its clearing it again took over two and a half hours, but the actual period of totality was five minutes 45 seconds. By moving in search of clear skies we had unfortunately forfeited a precious minute of the totality. The ship was 300 miles off the coast of Mauretania. All possible machinery was shut down, lights were turned off and we drifted in a calm sea, while our scientists, professional and amateur, pointed their battery of cameras, telescopes and other instruments at the dying sun. The open decks were an incredible sight, a virtual forest of tripods. As totality approached it began to grow dark and there was a noticeable drop in temperature. All colour was drained from the sea and sky. To me the supreme moment was when the sun suddenly shot out again like a beacon. All of us in *Canberra* were privileged to have seen an unforgettable sight.'

Meanwhile, as the newspaper headlines in Britain reported the early demise of the great liner, which in 1961 had been hailed as, 'the finest ship built in this country for years', the New York cruise programme continued. On the morning of 12 July, as *Canberra* was approaching the anchorage at St. George, Grenada, she went aground on a reef to the south of the harbour and stuck fast on sand and dead coral. The next day, whilst tugs were attempting to refloat her, a laundryman on board *Canberra* was killed when a steel hawser snapped and struck him on the head. Three days after grounding, during the afternoon of 15 July, the ship was refloated and the passengers were able to continue the cruise, which was concluded in New York on 20 July, two days late.

Just over three weeks later, during Tuesday 14 August, P&O suddenly announced that the *Canberra* was not going to be withdrawn after all as, '.... the growing demand for "open class" cruises - where passengers have the freedom of all public areas on board the ship - has led the company to amend its plans.' However, even though bookings for cruises had doubled during the summer of 1973, the New York experiment had not been a success and the liner was to be transferred to the company's UK-based programme for 1974. As if in response to the controversy, that same evening in St. Thomas, US Virgin Islands, the *Canberra* made her own protest as she ran aground once again. She was on an eight-day cruise from New York and at anchor when a sudden squall drove her onto a sandbank. With her port side, including the stabilizer, port propeller and her rudder embedded in soft coral, she took on a 2° list to starboard. That night she lay with her stern due east of Sprat Point, to the south-east of Water Island, with only 19ft of water at her lee side, but the following evening, at high water, she refloated herself. She suffered some scraping to her bottom and the tips of the port propeller blades were bent, but approval was given for repairs to be carried out during her next dry docking and she was, once again, able to continue on the cruise without too much delay.

The remainder of the US cruise programme passed without mishap and, having found a new role, her future seemed to be secure.

An unusual view of the *Canberra* at Southampton's Ocean Terminal in 1980, shortly before leaving for a summer cruise.   *(N. McCart)*

The *Canberra* returns to Southampton from the South Atlantic. Note the Wessex helicopter of the Queen's Flight on the midships flight deck.   *(N. McCart)*

Chapter Five

The Enemy In The South Atlantic

The conversion of the *Canberra* to a one-class ship was a fairly straightforward operation and proved more successful than with the *Oriana,* which had a more complicated internal design. The two ships were to be 'running mates' for the next eight years, operating from the UK between April and December, then the *Canberra* would undertake a world cruise during the winter months while the *Oriana* cruised out of Sydney. The *Canberra* began by taking over the *Orsova's* 1974 cruise programme, starting with the world cruise in January 1974 when she sailed via Madeira to Florida then Panama, across the Pacific to Auckland and Sydney, returning by way of Cape Town and the Canary Isles. It was to be a familiar pattern, although initially, with the massive rise in fuel costs and the long term future of cruising in doubt, plans were only made from year to year. However, despite steep increases in the cost of fares, the demand for P&O's unique holidays at sea continued to grow.

Although a typical first class passenger of the 1930s might flinch at the sight of some of the modern cabaret acts, the bingo sessions and the disco, they would still recognize the bridge clubs, the foxtrots and afternoon tea. The deck games, one imagines, are not very different from those played on the *Viceroy of India* in the 1930s, although with stabilizers the conditions are smoother. However, to keep over 1,000 passengers amused, keep fit classes, games contests (which used to be organized by a passengers' committee), classical concerts, fancy dress competitions, port lectures, and much more are all arranged by a cruise director. Even so, many people still prefer to spend their days contemplating the sea from deck chairs. Having been designed for fast voyages to Australia with powerful propulsion machinery, the *Canberra* uses a lot of fuel so she cruises at about 18 or 19 knots and, in order to make as many cruises as possible and stay profitable, a new cruise starts on the same day that the previous one ends. Departing passengers disembark in pre-arranged groups and only six or seven hours later a fresh company goes aboard the completely restocked vessel, which has been spruced to a pristine freshness. It all calls for a great deal of hard work from every member of the ship's company.

During the course of the 1970s, even in inflation-hit Britain, the cruising scene for the *Canberra* continued to

On 7 April 1982 preparations were urgently under way to prepare *Canberra* for her voyage as a troop transport to the Falkland Islands. Here she lies alongside 105 berth and the two helicopter flight decks are being completed.

(P&O)

improve. In late 1976 P&O were able to announce that 1,200 passengers had booked for the 1977 world cruise, which was 100 more than the previous year, and bookings were being made for 1978. It was encouraging that in 1976 the passenger division showed a good profit, which was in contrast to a £6 million loss for 1975.

By 1981 the *Canberra's* 'Christmas Cruise' followed by her round-the-world voyage had become a tradition at P&O Cruises and on Saturday 12 December 1981 she left Southampton for a 24-night voyage to Tenerife, Barbados, Martinique, Port Everglades and Madeira, before returning home on 5 January 1982. The passengers enjoyed a Christmas in the best British tradition, with the added bonus of the tropical sun. A Christmas tree was fixed to the mast, carols were sung and Father Christmas accompanied King Neptune at the 'Crossing the Line' ceremony. It was a festive end to a year which had seen a lot of disruptive industrial action by dock workers at Southampton which, on one occasion, meant the ship had to anchor off Spithead and land her passengers by tender.

The day after she completed the Christmas cruise, the *Canberra* left Southampton for her 1982 world cruise, which was described as: 'One of the world's great adventures - 90 days away from winter.' With her first call being Madeira, she then steamed west to Bermuda, Port Everglades and Panama. As she passed through the waterway on 22 January 1982 few, if any, passengers or crew members would have given much thought to the deteriorating relationship between Britain and Argentina over the future of the Falkland Islands.

By 8 March the British government were so concerned by the Argentinian threat to the islands that the Ministry of Defence were approached about sending warships to the area, and later that month the unauthorized appearance of an Argentinian naval ice-breaker and scrap-metal merchant at Grytviken, South Georgia, started to make headlines in the British press. By 20 March 1982, it had become clear that there was some collusion between the scrap-dealer and the Argentinian Navy in order to establish a presence on the island, and the crew from the Argentinian naval support vessel *Bahia Buen Sucesco,* which had anchored in Leith Harbour, raised an Argentinian flag, at which time the *Canberra* was a long way away at the Seychelles in the Indian Ocean. As the days progressed, the political situation continued to worsen, and on 2 April 1982 the Argentinians invaded the Falkland Islands, an action which was rightly described by the British government as, 'an act of uprovoked aggression.'

On 18 March 1982 the Chief of the Naval Staff in London had been instructed to prepare, 'a task force likely to be capable of retaking the islands.' On the day of the flag-raising, the *Canberra* was in Athens, and on 2 April she was in Naples, only five days away from the end of her world cruise. That same day P&O managers in London were called to the Ministry of Defence where they were informed that the *Canberra* was likely to be requisitioned by the government and two days later, when the liner was off Gibraltar, a message was received on board to the effect that she had, in fact, been taken over by the government.

The *Canberra* refuels at sea from an RFA tanker as she steams south with the task force. *(P&O)*

On 27 January 1982, as the *Canberra* left Acapulco for San Francisco, the Argentine government delivered a paper to Britain's Ambassador in that country setting out the Argentinian claim to the Falkland Islands, and over the following weeks, whilst *Canberra* was in the Pacific Ocean, the position continued to deteriorate.

Meanwhile, staff at P&O Cruises were sending out notices to those passengers who were booked on *Canberra's* cruise 201, which had been due to sail for a nine-day cruise to Vigo, Ibiza and Palma, telling them that it had been cancelled, and it was not long before cruises 202 and 203, to West Africa and the Mediterranean, were also cancelled. At

7.30am on Wednesday 7 April 1982, the *Canberra* tied up alongside 106 berth at Southampton Docks and her passengers were soon starting to disembark. Later that day preparations were begun to convert the liner into a troop transport.*

For two days the workmen from Vosper's worked to build two helicopter flight decks, one over the forward observation deck and one above the midships Bonito swimming-pool. By midday on 8 April the first two and a half thousand troops had embarked and on the following day at 8.15pm, just over 60 hours after completing her world cruise, *Canberra* left Southampton for the South Atlantic, cheered on her way by thousands of well-wishers. As the ship steamed south, workmen from Vosper's continued their work to complete the forward flight deck and the troops trained relentlessly, causing the Promenade Deck to shudder under their feet as they jogged around it. One week later, on Saturday 17 April, the *Canberra* berthed alongside a small pier in Freetown, a port used regularly by troopships in the Second World War, where she took on fuel, water and stores. At midnight, with the fuelling operation completed, she left Freetown and three days later arrived off Ascension Island, where she was to remain for 17 days while the politicians attempted to work out a 'diplomatic' solution.

In early May the campaign at sea started in earnest when the submarine HMS *Conquerer* torpedoed and sank the cruiser *General Belgrano,* which had posed a particularly dangerous threat to the task force, and then HMS *Sheffield* was hit

Ships of the task force, including *HMS Fearless* and the *Canberra*, anchored off Ascension Island during their voyage south to the Falkland Islands. *(P&O)*

by air-launched Exocet missiles. By 8 May aircraft and warships from the task force were bombarding Argentinian positions on the Falklands, and by now the *Canberra* was 570 miles south-west by south of Ascension Island, having left two days previously with the MV *Elk* and HMS *Ardent*. On 10 May the vessels rendezvoused with the assault ships *Fearless*

The *Canberra* anchored at San Carlos Water on Friday 21 May 1982. The first Argentinian air attacks started at 8.05 am and continued throughout the day until 4 pm. *(P&O)*

* The last P&O liner to be used as a troopship was the *Strathnaver,* which had been released from government service in November 1948, just over 33 years previously.

and *Intrepid,* the *Atlantic Conveyor, Europic Ferry* and the RFA *Stromness,* 1,000 miles north-west of Tristan da Cunha. Six days later the convoy joined other warships and auxiliaries 650 miles from the Falkland Islands, and on 18 May they rendezvoused with the aircraft-carrier HMS *Hermes.*

At 10pm on Thursday 20 May 1982 general emergency stations were sounded as the *Canberra* and the other vessels made their final approach to the islands, through the narrow and dangerous waters of the Falkland Sound. At just after midnight on Friday 21 May she anchored off Fanning Head where most of the troops disembarked, and at just after 6am she anchored in San Carlos Water. The first Argentinian air attacks started at 8.50am that morning and continued all day until 4pm, keeping the *Canberra's* anti-aircraft gunners, who were armed with general purpose machine-guns affixed to the guard rails, very busy. That evening, having safely disembarked the reserve units on board, the *Canberra* weighed anchor and set course for a position about 130 miles north-north-east of Port Stanley.

For three days the *Canberra* steamed off the north-east coast of the islands and during the afternoon of 25 May, in company with the *Norland,* left for South Georgia where she was to meet up with the *QE2,* which had also been requisitioned. In the early hours of 27 May icebergs were sighted and speed was reduced and later in the day she anchored at Grytviken, a most unusual setting for a vessel which had been built for tropical waters. In the evening the *QE2* arrived, having been delayed by ice and fog, and almost immediately the transfer of personnel and stores began. Late on 28 May, the day that Goose Green and Darwin were captured from the Argentinians, the *Canberra* left South Georgia, bound once again for San Carlos, where she arrived on a dull and foggy Wednesday 2 June.

By this time, with British troops poised to retake Port Stanley, the final outcome of the campaign was not in any doubt, but it was a relief to all on board when *Canberra* left San Carlos the following day, because the Argentinian Air Force was still a very potent threat. The Argentinian garrison finally surrendered on 14 June 1982 and at about 7pm that day the *Canberra* was ordered back to San Carlos Water, this time to embark Argentinian POWs. One hundred men of the Welsh Guards came on board to act as guards and the plan was to allocate the whole of the ship from B Deck downwards to the prisoners with guards posted at the end of every passageway and on each staircase. Once embarked, the POWs were taken to the Meridian Room where they were searched, before being directed to a space on board. By the evening of 15 June there were 1,121 POWs on board and on the following day the liner moved round to Port William* to embark a further 3,046 Argentinian prisoners. These men were assembled on A Deck to be searched, and they were described as being, '.... very little trouble. The great majority are only too delighted to be warm, dry, well fed and on their way home.' On the morning of 18 June, with the vessel having been guaranteed a safe passage, the

11 July 1982, a glorious summer's day, and the *Canberra* returns to Southampton. Here she is seen off 38/39 berth, with the Wessex helicopter piloted by the Prince of Wales on the Sun Deck, and the Royal Marine Band on the forward flight deck. *(P&O)*

Canberra left Port William for Puerto Madryn, Argentina. On the afternoon of the next day, with the Argentinian flag at the mast-head in accordance with normal practice, the *Canberra* berthed alongside an ore jetty and disembarkation of the prisoners began. The first to leave were the 'walking wounded' who received some applause, but as the disembarkation gathered momentum the Argentinian welcoming party, which included a general, left the jetty. One eyewitness observed that the 200 or so Argentinian officers were, 'busy saluting one another' and the prisoners' reception was very subdued. In just over four hours, with all the prisoners ashore, the *Canberra* left Puerto Madryn for Port Stanley, where it was thought she would embark more POWs.

However, after anchoring at Port William, it was announced that the ship would be returning home with men of 40 and 42 Commando, Royal Marines. The *Canberra* finally left the Falkland Islands at 5.22pm on 25 June 1982 for a much more relaxed voyage home.

The *Canberra's* return to Southampton on Sunday 11 July, a glorious summer's day, was a momentous occasion. Every vantage point on the banks of the Solent, Southampton Water and the city itself was packed with people all cheering the 'Great White Whale' as she had become known. As she approached the quayside she was completely surrounded by masses of small boats, and as she neared 106 berth the Royal Marine band struck up 'Land of Hope and Glory' accompanied by all the Marines on board and the huge crowds that packed Southampton Docks. She had steamed 25,245 nautical miles, and had the honour of landing most of the ground forces who went into action during the campaign. The nation had taken the great ship to its heart.

However, now that it was all over, the time had come to restore the 'weather-beaten' liner to her former pristine condition so that she could return to her true role once again.

*It was at Port William that Admiral Sturdee's fleet first sighted Admiral von Spee's squadron in December 1914. The British fleet then included the auxiliary cruiser HMS *Macedonia,* which was a converted P&O liner. The *Macedonia's* contribution to this first Battle of the Falkland Islands was to intercept and sink two German transports and to take their crews on board as POWs .

Chapter Six

Cruises To The Sun

Although the *Canberra* suffered no structural damage during 'Operation Corporate', she had been subjected to a great deal of wear and tear and her usually gleaming white livery was streaked with rust.

(N. McCart)

Although the *Canberra* had suffered no structural damage during 'Operation Corporate', she had been subjected to a great deal of wear and tear and her usual gleaming white livery was streaked with rust. In addition of course, the areas which had been altered in order to accommodate the two helicopter flight decks had to be restored to their original design and all the passenger accommodation had to be refurbished. The cost of most of the work was met by the government, but during the refit P&O made some improvements to the public rooms which were financed by the company. The most noticeable of these was the addition of a bar on the starboard side of the Island Room and another was the instal-

lation of air-conditioning in the Stadium. By the end of the first week in September the *Canberra* looked as good as new, with her hull repainted, and she was ready to depart on her first Mediterranean cruise of the season. It was 11 September, a warm, sunny day and huge crowds in the port of Southampton gave her a warm send-off, while a fireboat and the training ship *Malcolm Miller* escorted her down Southampton Water. For P&O it was a great relief to get the *Canberra* back to her normal role for, although the government's charter rates had ensured that the company suffered no financial loss, passengers had turned to other shipping lines for their summer holiday cruises.

With her white hull returned to its usual pristine condition, the *Canberra* is ready to sail for another cruise. *(N. McCart)*

The *Canberra* completed her remaining cruises on 22 October 1982 and as soon as her passengers had disembarked she went into Southampton's No. 7 dry dock for a further refit. Although it was only five weeks since she had finished her nine-week overhaul, not all the annual survey work had been completed during that time. However, as the inspection of the underwater hull and propellers had already been carried out, she remained afloat and Vosper's were able to use their excellent cranage facilities. After the refit she sailed for Australia on Saturday 13 November 1982, three days late, which was due to a minor fire during the overhaul, but she was able to make up much of the lost time during the voyage and she was only one day late when she arrived in Sydney on 22 December for a two-month cruising season.

By 15 April 1983 she was back cruising from Southampton and during the year bookings increased by 30% which, although partly due to cancelled cruises from the previous year, was a good sign for the future. At the end of 1983 the *Canberra's* annual overhaul was carried out in Germany and during 1984 industrial problems at Southampton greatly inconvenienced both the company and passengers, and so it was inevitable that the annual overhaul would continue to be awarded to German shipyards.

In November 1986, following the withdrawal of the *Oriana* earlier in the year, the *Canberra*, which was now 25 years old, was completely refurbished at the Lloyd Werft shipyard at Bremerhaven. During the refit the Pacific Restaurant was fitted with new furnishings and the Atlantic Restaurant was also redesigned and refurbished. The Meridian Room was completely refurnished and laid out to provide a comfortable lounge for concerts and quiet relaxation. The William Fawcett Room was redesigned and renamed the Ocean Room (which is the name which had originally been intend-

August 1989, and the *Canberra* is making a lot of black smoke. *(N. McCart)*

ed in 1960 for, what was then, the tourist class lounge). Right aft the Peacock Room, which was once the tourist class smoking room, was renamed Neptune's and during daylight hours it is a light and pleasant room with windows giving aquatic views of the Alice Springs pool, while in the evenings it is transformed into a lively night-club. In the Island Room a full buffet was installed, making refreshments available for 18 hours a day. Carpeting was fitted along the passageways on A, B, Promenade and C Decks which completely transformed those areas. All the accommodation on G Deck was given over to the professional theatre players, and the Stadium Theatre itself was fitted with permanent tiered seating for the gala shows and variety performances. The ship was now set for the 1990s and the last decade of the 20th century.

and a launderette, all of which were kept scrupulously clean.

Owing to the late tide we departed at 10pm that evening and, despite the fact that darkness had fallen, the farewell was just as exciting, with the band playing on the quayside and streamers in abundance. Monday 7 August dawned as a clear, bright day, with the temperature rising as the ship approached Ushant and the Bay of Biscay. At breakfast time passengers can choose the traditional waiter service in the restaurants or the popular self-service buffet in the Island Room. The Bay of Biscay was on its best behaviour that day and with the sun shining it was a marvellous start to the cruise.

That afternoon, as we relaxed beside the Lido pool, aft on the Games Deck, we were fortunate enough to see an Orca whale breaching off our port quarter. For those passengers

During her well publicized 'Sunshine & Cities' cruise around the Mediterranean in August 1989, one port of call was Elba. In this view she is anchored off Portoferraio on a searingly hot day.
(N. McCart)

By the late 1980s *Canberra's* cruises were legendary in the leisure industry and one such well publicized voyage in August 1989 took her on a 'Sunshine and Cities' cruise to Gibraltar, the French Riviera, Livorno, San Remo, Elba and Vigo, and the sunshine was in abundance as one passenger recalls: 'Although we have cruised aboard *Canberra* a number of times, there is always that feeling of anticipation and excitement as one gets near to the reception lounge at the P&O berth. At the foot of the gangway one of the ship's stewards took our hand luggage and guided us from the gangway foyer on D Deck to our cabin which was situated on the starboard side of C Deck aft. It was a compact four-berth room with two lower and two upper bunks, plenty of drawer and wardrobe space, a wash-basin and a picture window. Just around the corner were showers, a bath, toilets

who preferred to stay below decks, the 'indoor' activities had begun with dancing and art classes, bingo and table tennis. On the Sun Deck the devoted sun worshippers had already staked out their places beside the Bonito Pool, but it was pleasant sitting in the shade and watching the sea and the world go by.

It was with excitement that I anticipated our first port of call, Gibraltar, for I had last visited the colony 20 years ago to the month when serving aboard the aircraft-carrier HMS *Eagle,* and to my delight the *Canberra* tied up alongside the same berth which the *Eagle* had used all those years ago. However, with the younger members of our family anxious to get to a beach, we took a bumpy but friendly bus ride to Main Street and then a short journey by taxi to Catalan Bay, directly beneath the water catchments. Upon departure at

6pm that day, the *Canberra* was manoeuvred out of the confines of the harbour and then navigated close to the eastern shoreline of the Rock, before an easterly course was set across the Alboran Sea for Toulon. The following day saw *Canberra* on an east-north-easterly course with calm seas and a clear blue sky. At lunchtime landfall was made off Ibiza's Espart Island, and for nearly two hours the ship navigated close in to the shore. Later that afternoon we emerged from the

Canberra's Sun Deck lives up to its name while the ship is anchored off Elba in August 1989.   *(N. McCart)*

In recent years the *Canberra* has undergone her annual refit in Germany and here she is shown arriving at Bremerhaven.   *(R. Witthohn)*

The *Canberra* anchored at Santorini, Greece, on 13 September 1992. In the foreground is the barque-rigged motor vessel *Sea Cloud* which was built in Germany in 1931 as the *Hussar*.
(*W. A. Cole*)

children's disco in the Island Room to view the magnificent sight of Majorca's rocky and rugged northern coastline, about a mile away on our starboard side. That evening, as the *Canberra* steamed steadily north-east across the Gulf of Lions, the sky astern was brilliantly lit by two separate electrical storms on the horizon, an awe-inspiring sight.

After a blistering hot day on the Cote d' Azure, the *Canberra* made an overnight passage across the Ligurian Sea to berth in the Italian port of Livorno (Leghorn). It is Italy's third largest seaport, but the main attractions for passengers were trips to Pisa and Florence. One of my most vivid memories is of the famous bell-tower, almost 14 ft out of perpendicular. That same evening on the Ligurian Sea, between Livorno and San Remo, on a bright moonlit night with a sea as calm as a millpond, the ship was stopped for an hour or more for the festivities of Island Night, which was brought to a close with a mass rendition of "Land of Hope and Glory."

The next day saw us anchored off San Remo, the Italian resort in the province of Imperia, and I know that we will always treasure our memories of this lovely town with its profusion of palms and flowers. At midnight *Canberra* left the twinkling lights of San Remo behind and made yet another overnight crossing, this time to Portoferraio on the island of Elba. Unfortunately it was one of the very few days of the year when Napoleon's villa was closed, but the busy little town was most interesting.

After leaving Elba *Canberra* steamed south and at midnight she transited the Bonifacio Strait between Corsica and Sardinia, with the lights of Cape Testa on the latter island being clearly visible. By 10am the next day we had reached Cape Cabellerio on Menorca's northern shore and for the rest of the morning we cruised along the island's north and west coasts, before picking up Majorca's south-eastern shore at 1pm. For two hours *Canberra* close navigated off this coast, passing several of the resort towns which looked like incongruous concrete jungles on an otherwise beautiful island.

By 4am on 16 August *Canberra* had rounded Cape de Gata, this time westbound, and set a west-south-westerly course towards the Straits of Gibraltar. At 11am we passed just south of Europa Point, with the other 'Pillar of Hercules' clearly visible through the mists which hung over the Rif mountains of Morocco. Our final port of call was Vigo, Spain's major port on the Atlantic coast.'

This passenger perhaps sums up what many people have thought about P&O's last mail ship: 'On the last day of the cruise, as I stood at the after end of the Promenade Deck watching *Canberra's* twin screws endlessly churning up the calm waters of the Bay of Biscay, I wondered how much longer this unique ship would carry Britain's holiday-makers to the sun.'

Chapter Seven

Sea Princess - An Inauspicious Start

The *Kungsholm* on the stocks at John Brown's Clydebank shipyard.   *(Scottish Record Office)*

One of the most prestigious shipping lines on the North Atlantic, in terms of comfort and quality, was the Swedish-America Line, whose origins go back to 1915, the first full year of the First World War. In that year the Rederie Sverige Nordamerika Company purchased a 12,600-ton Dutch liner, renamed her *Stockholm* and put her on the Gothenburg-New York route. In March 1922 the company became known as the Swedish-America Line and that same year they bought another Dutch liner, the *Noordam,* and she became the first *Kungsholm.* She was sold two years later and in 1928 the second vessel to bear the name entered service. She remained on the route between Gothenburg and New York until the Second World War when trade on the Atlantic ceased. The third *Kungsholm,* a 21,141-ton motor vessel, was built in 1953 and she remained in the company's service for only 11 years before being sold to North German Lloyd, who renamed her *Europa.* She survived until July 1984 when she struck the breakwater in Cadiz harbour and sank.

In the early 1960s the general trend in North Atlantic travel showed a declining number of passengers crossing by sea. More and more vessels were employed in the cruise trade, not only in the low season, but also in mid-summer. The *Kungsholm* of 1953 had been built specifically for the transatlantic trade at a time when the idea of carrying hundreds of people in aircraft was never taken too seriously. Although

she could, if really necessary, be used for cruising, she was really an Atlantic liner. It was this vessel's limited capabilities which, in late 1962, led the directors of the Swedish-America Line to plan a replacement for the liner when she was only nine years old. In December 1962 the company invited tenders from European shipyards for a 26,000-ton passenger vessel, which would be designed with cruising in mind.

Almost immediately attention was focused on a number of British shipyards, and prominent among these was the Clydeside company of John Brown. The last passenger liner which had been built at a British shipyard was the *Northern Star* and she had been handed over to Shaw Savill in June 1962. The fitting out of this vessel had been plagued by industrial disputes and at John Brown's yard on Clydeside morale was depressed by continual industrial problems and the failure to win orders. Lord Aberconway, the Chairman of John Brown & Co., spoke at a shareholders' meeting of the 'quite unprecedented' situation in the company, at any rate since 1931, which with the launching of a BP tanker and of Blue Funnel's *Centaur* that year, left only two ships on order still to launch. This situation had come about despite the most resolute efforts to secure further work, and to this end prices quoted by the company had been well below cost price. For all at John Brown's this dearth of orders was distressing and so, with the announcement of the proposed

Scandinavian liner, great efforts were made to secure the contract.

In the summer of 1963 John Rannie, the Sales and Deputy Managing Director of John Brown & Co., together with other company directors including Mr John Brown, spent weeks in Gothenburg working hard to persuade the directors of the Swedish-America Line to have their new passenger ship built on the Clyde. It was not an easy task for there were two rival bids from British shipyards and two from shipyards on the continent, but, on 22 August 1963, Mr E. Christiansson, the Technical Director of the Swedish-America Line, announced that the order had indeed gone to John Brown & Co. He also said that, although the new ship was to be designed especially for cruising in tropical waters, her appearance would be very similar to that of the company's vessels *Gripsholm* (23,191grt) and the third *Kungsholm* (21,141grt). He also stated that the contract had gone to John Brown & Co., because of '.... the fact that their delivery time is considerably shorter', which was a very important factor in their decision. It was announced that they wanted building to start at the beginning of 1963 and delivery to take place in the last quarter of 1965. Although the final contract price had not been fixed, since the Swedish company had an option of choice in respect of sub-contracts, it was known to be close to £7 million.

It was a vital order for John Brown & Co. at a time of high unemployment in the area, for not only did it involve a large passenger liner, but it was also the most valuable overseas order for a single merchant ship ever received. The fulfilment of the contract meant that a number of planned redundancies within the company could be cancelled and, although there was to be no large scale recruitment, extra skilled tradesmen would be taken on.

The directors of John Brown's had made a prolonged study of the requirements of the Swedish-America Line and this included a special visit to the *Gripsholm* to view one of their vessels at first hand. They were able to publicly announce: 'Our success in winning this order demonstrates John Brown's ability to compete in the international market, particularly for liners and specialist ships', but privately within the management there was some concern, for the price quoted to the Swedish-America Line left very little, if any, margin for profit.

However, planning and design work started almost immediately and five months later the keel for yard number 728 was laid at No. 3 berth in the Clydebank shipyard. It was a

The launching of the new Scandinavian liner took place on Wednesday 14 April 1965, with the naming ceremony being performed by Mrs Dan-Axel Brostrom, wife of the Chairman of the Swedish-America Line.

(Scottish Record Office)

With the launching ceremony over, the *Kungsholm* is towed to her fitting-out berth at Clydebank. *(Scottish Record Office)*

slipway which had seen the construction of some other very notable vessels, including the battleship *HMS Vanguard*, the Cunard liner *Caronia* and P&O's *Arcadia*.

As the new ship took shape on the Clyde, the builders were bedevilled by a series of problems which caused great anxiety to the directors of the company. Most of the trouble stemmed from a shortage of skilled labour at the yard, which caused the gap between the contracted date and the actual completion date to grow wider, and added to this was the overspending on the planned budget. Well before the half-way stage had been reached, over half of the money which had been set aside had been used. It was becoming clear that not only would the delivery of the vessel be delayed, but there would be no profit for John Brown's, who might even incur a loss.

Gone were the days when, at the turn of the century, British shipbuilders had produced well over half of the world's shipping. By the early 1960s there was an upsurge of competition from European companies and, in the case of passenger liners, there was the additional uncertainty about competition from the airlines.

The launching of the new Scandinavian liner took place on Wednesday 14 April 1965 with the naming ceremony being performed by Mrs Dan-Axel Brostrom, the wife of the Chairman of the Swedish-America Line. Although it was a happy occasion, the difficulties which faced this great shipbuilding company were never far below the surface, even though four months previously they had also gained the contract to build the *QE2*. In his speech following the ceremony,

Mr John Rannie referred to the inflexible attitudes of trade unions, whose rigid demarcation policies would not allow for the interchanging and temporary upgrading of workers in the industry, which he blamed for the skill shortages. Lord Aberconway pointed out to the guests that the *Kungsholm* was the first ship to be built at Clydebank for Sweden in living memory. Mr Erik Wijk, Managing Director of the Swedish-America Line, spoke optimistically of the possibility of a sister ship for the *Kungsholm,* for even then no one could foresee the rapid collapse of passenger shipping on the North Atlantic, with only a gradual increase in the popularity of cruising.

Originally the *Kungsholm* was to have been delivered to her owners in November 1965, but when that date came round there was still a great deal of fitting out work to be completed and it was to be another four months before she would be ready for handing over. However, the directors of the Swedish-America Line requested that preliminary trials be carried out and so, in mid-November, satisfactory basin trials of her machinery were conducted. Then on Friday 19 November she left the Clyde to carry out stability tests, steering gear trials and speed runs over the measured mile off Arran. On board the trials party consisted of over 200 directors, management staff and technicians from the Swedish-America Line, who were to examine every aspect of the vessel's performance in great detail. Two days later, with all the tests successfully completed, the *Kungsholm* returned to the builder's yard for the tradesmen to complete the installation of the furnishings and fittings.

The *Sea Princess* leaves Southampton on the evening of 7 August 1982 for a 13-night cruise to the Northern Capitals. Forward of her the *Canberra* can be seen still undergoing her overhaul, having returned from the South Atlantic just four weeks previously. *(N. McCart)*

The *Sea Princess* in the Mediterranean. *(P&O Cruises)*

Chapter Eight

Scandinavian Influence In Interior Design

Despite the financial difficulties which faced John Brown & Co., there is no doubt that, in the best traditions of this distinguished company, they had built a fine new ship. The *Kungsholm* was a vessel with a pleasing and graceful appearance both externally and internally. Her owners had chosen an unashamedly traditional design with a clipper bow, two raked aluminium masts, a cruiser stern and two funnels which really looked like funnels, even though the forward one was actually a dummy. She had a white hull livery and the pale yellow funnels carried the owner's crest of a blue circle with three crowns.

Her hull form was the result of extensive tests carried out at the National Physical Laboratory at Feltham. She was the first Scandinavian passenger vessel to be fitted with a bulbous bow, a feature proposed by the builders, and it is interesting to compare this decision with that arrived at by the owners of the *Sagafjord*, completed in May 1965, who considered that while improving performance at service speeds on the North Atlantic route, it would have the opposite effect at operational speeds as a cruise ship. However, as both ships

The enclosed promenade on the Lido Deck. This view was taken on the port side looking forward. *(K. Vard)*

The Starlight Lounge at the forward end of the Lido Deck. Originally this was the Observation Lounge and, with its adjoining verandahs on the port and starboard sides, it provides passengers with a comfortable area for relaxation. *(K. Vard)*

are still successfully in service it cannot have made that much difference.

The *Kungsholm* was designed to carry 750 transatlantic passengers in two classes when she was in service between Gothenburg and New York, but in her cruising role this

number was reduced to 450. She also carried a complement of 438 officers and crew members. The owners enlisted the services of a number of Swedish and British designers for the public rooms, and their work was co-ordinated by Robert Tillberg, a leading Swedish marine interior designer. However, the actual work of interior decoration was supervised by a London company, Tabb Haslehurst Ltd., who were responsible for the production of all working drawings and who also designed the auditorium, the forward writing room and library, together with both swimming-pools and the main foyers and stairways.

The passenger accommodation is on seven decks from the Sun Deck, down through the Promenade, Verandah, Upper, A, B, and C Decks. Most of the public rooms are on the Promenade and Verandah Decks. On the Promenade Deck forward there was the Observation Lounge, which is now called the Starlight Lounge. This room was designed by Count Bernadotte and, with its adjoining verandahs on the port and starboard sides, it still provides passengers with a comfortable area for relaxation by day, or a night-club. Originally the combined area could seat 110 people at buffet luncheons, and the design encouraged a shipboard atmosphere with large picture windows which enabled passengers to enjoy the sea views. French windows open out onto the enclosed verandahs and mahogany panelled bulkheads blend with soft decorative colours. In the main lounge area, which looks forward from the bridge front, there is a raised section forward, which is fitted with a gyro repeater-compass which is connected to the bridge. On either side of this section there are brass-framed portholes which look onto the port and starboard verandahs. In the main section there is a grand piano and a rosewood dance floor. Originally the furniture in the room was of a contemporary Danish design.

Moving aft through enclosed promenades on both sides of the ship, the lido area is reached amidships in the space

The Lido area soon after the vessel was taken over by P&O. *(N. McCart)*

which was originally between the two funnels. At Sun Deck level there was a wide, screened solarium, and exterior stairways on both port and starboard sides descended to a covered terrace, which in turn was raised above and forward of the swimming-pool area. Steps from the terrace descended aft to the swimming-pool at Promenade Deck level and a line of folding screens enabled the area to be protected from the wind. The lido area has since been redesigned and it is virtually unrecognizable now.

The top of the main stairway and the two main passenger lifts rise immediately aft of the swimming-pool and they are separated from it by a glass-fronted lobby. There were originally two enclosed promenades outboard, leading aft from the lido area, which terminated in exterior staircases down to the Verandah Deck. Between these two promenades was the Sports Room which served a dual purpose as an indoor games room and a children's nursery. It was built with a large overhead dome in the centre to give additional height for indoor games to be played. Although the Sports Room has gone, the raised dome roof is still there, in what is now the Carib Lounge. Today's passengers have the use of an additional swimming-pool which has been added aft of this lounge.

At the forward end of the Verandah Deck was the *Kungsholm's* 307-seat auditorium which was originally designed as a combined cinema, theatre and lecture hall, and which is now the Princess Theatre. A cinema screen can be lowered for film or slide projection and at the forward end there is the

projection room from which lights, sound relaying equipment and film projection are controlled. One of the interesting features of this system is its flexibility, which allows films to be simultaneously relayed to television sets in passengers' and officers' cabins. The raised section at the after end was originally designed so that it could be easily separated from the rest of the room and be used by first class passengers when the ship was on the North Atlantic, leaving the remaining part to the tourist class.

The Carousel Room on the *Sea Princess* in 1982. This room was built where the old tourist class Sports Room used to be at the after end of the Promenade Deck, now the Lido Deck. *(N. McCart)*

The library on the port side of R Deck, forward. This room was originally designed in an 'antique' English style.   (N. McCart)

On the port side of the auditorium is the forward writing room and library, which was designed in an 'antique' English style with heavy yew wood panelling, while the hardwood furniture was in a traditional Scandinavian design. Today the library is little changed from those early days and it retains its original ambience. Aft of the library on the port side was the Cocktail Lounge which was designed by Mr R. Aberg who employed rosewood panelling throughout. He also made impressive use of slatted screens, lighting and mirrors on either side of the bar which created a focal point here, and the renamed Riviera Bar is still very much as it was nearly 30 years ago. On the starboard side of the theatre is the Princess Boutique, occupying the area which was formerly the card-room, enclosed verandah and shop.

Situated aft of the main staircase on the Verandah Deck is the main lounge, which was designed by Robert Tillberg. It was the tourist class lounge whilst on the North Atlantic, but open to all passengers when cruising. At 6,400 square feet and extending over the full width of the ship, it is a large room which was originally panelled in dyed beechwood with predominantly gold decoration. An unusual feature of the room is a central raised section of the deckhead which was at one time covered in gold leaf. At the forward end there is an extending stage which is concealed when not in use by sliding metal gates in front of curtains. Movable seating is situated on three sides of the rosewood dance floor and settees are placed in the alcoves which are formed by raised sections of deck at the sides of the room. Today the International Lounge provides the main rendezvous for shipboard entertainment during cruises.

The after cocktail lounge and smoking room, which used to be on the Verandah Deck (now R Deck). This room was replaced by an extra 80 cabins during the 1978/79 conversion for P&O.   (Author's collection)

At the after end of the Verandah Deck the Verandah Lounge opened onto the adjoining smoking room. The port side of the lounge was panelled in light grey oak, and there was a dance floor in the raised after section of the room. However, this combined lounge and smoking room no longer exists and in its place are 80 extra cabins, most of

The Pacific Lounge on the Verandah Deck in 1982. It is now the International Lounge on R Deck. In this photograph the sliding metal gates which conceal the extending stage can be seen.

(N. McCart)

which are twin-bedded rooms, apart from two which are single-berth cabins.

The main dining saloon, designed by R. Aberg, is on A Deck and access to it is from either the forward or the main midships staircase. It is a large compartment which originally allowed more than 16 square feet of space for each of the 500 seats. Waist-high, metal balustrades separate the main floor area from raised sections on either side of the room. The bulkhead panelling is in light cherrywood and centred in the after bulkhead is a carved mirror etched with construction drawings of ancient Swedish warships.

On cruises the 450 passengers were all accommodated in lower berths and on the Atlantic service the first class passengers all had cabins on the Upper Deck, whilst the tourist class passengers were in two-, three- and four-berth cabins on the Main, A and B Decks. Over 90% of the cabins had shower/bath and toilet facilities and each was fitted with its own telephone. All the passenger and crew accommodation was air-conditioned.

Like all the post-war Swedish-America Line vessels, the *Kungsholm* was a diesel-driven ship with twin screws which are powered by two Götaverken 760/1500 VG-9U series diesel engines capable of a combined normal continuous output of 25,200 BHP at 120 rpm. It was, at that time, the most powerful single installation undertaken by the Gothenburg engineering company and was designed for operation on heavy boiler fuel oil. The vessel's normal service speed was 21 knots at 80% power, but she was capable of a maximum sustained speed of 23 knots. In the auxiliary machinery space four oil-fired boilers were installed, which generate steam at 114 psi for a number of uses, including the ship's evaporating plant which can produce 360 tons of distilled water a day. Electrical power at 440V, 3-ph, 60c/sec is furnished by five 1,000 kVA diesel alternators - representing a maximum power capability of 4,000 kW. These are all powered by 6-cylinder Ruston & Hornsby diesel engines.

On the navigation bridge, the wheelhouse and chartroom were merged into one 'navigation centre' with two main consoles and the Sperry gyro-hydraulic steering control unit. The design of the bridge layout and the consoles was carried out by the builders.

In the words of Erik Wijk, Managing Director of the Swedish-America Line, the *Kungsholm* was, '... one of the finest we have ever received from any shipyard.'

Chapter Nine

The Scandinavian Princess

The *Kungsholm* at anchor in the Clyde during her official trials in March 1966.　　　　　*(Maritime Photo Library)*

The *Kungsholm* finally left John Brown's yard for her official trials on Friday 11 March 1966, when she moved down river from the fitting-out basin to the Tail of the Bank for the tests to begin. She was some four months behind schedule but, apart from some valuable murals and items of furniture, her fitting out had been completed. Fortunately everything went well and later the following day she was able to leave for dry docking at Belfast, before returning to the Tail of the Bank on the morning of Wednesday 16 March to complete the trials. The next day, having been handed over to the Swedish-America Line, she finally left the Clyde and set course via the Pentland Firth and the North Sea for Gothenburg.

Her arrival at the Stigbergskajen in her home port on Sunday 20 March 1966 was greeted by crowds of enthusiastic spectators. During her North Sea passage the *Kungsholm* had logged 25 knots, against the 24 knots which had been achieved on her trials and a contract speed of 21 knots. Despite the fact that she had encountered winds of 32 knots, she had behaved admirably with no ballast whatever on board. Her master, as well as the accompanying technical experts, commented that she was extremely 'sea kindly'. In praising the vessel and her builders, Mr Erik Wijk said: 'Her builders have spared no effort in meeting our very severe and minutely detailed specifications and we have got what we wanted - the finest passenger ship ever built. We are very proud of her and I feel my friends on the Clyde have reason

to share in our pride in spite of the unfortunate economic consequences arising out of the delays. I am also convinced that when we show our new flagship in New York our feelings about her will be fully shared by our very discriminating travelling public over there. She is in fact a wonderful ship.'

Over the next four weeks considerable amounts of furniture and valuable fittings were installed on board, and it was not until Friday 22 April 1966 that she was ready to make her maiden voyage to New York. Unfortunately the omens for the future were not at all good for, despite widespread publicity, only about 300 passengers had booked to travel in the new ship. The late 1950s had seen the numbers of those crossing the Atlantic by air growing by at least 100,000 a year, and in the early 1960s they outnumbered sea travellers on the route. By the mid-1960s all the shipping companies which operated transatlantic services were suffering large financial losses and it was looking increasingly unlikely that any passenger liner could make a profit there. However, the *Kungsholm* made her first Atlantic crossing by way of Copenhagen and the north coast of Scotland, and after a voyage of nine days, she arrived in New York on Monday 2 May, to the traditional welcome of sirens and fireboat water jets. Despite the rough seas, her passengers had nothing but praise for the *Kungsholm's* seagoing qualities.

After a three-day stop-over in New York the *Kungsholm* returned to Gothenburg by the same route, arriving back in her home port on Saturday 14 May. Later that month she

The *Kungsholm* at Wellington, New Zealand, during her first world cruise in 1967. With her clipper bow, two raked aluminium masts and two funnels which actually looked like funnels, she was a vessel with a pleasing and graceful appearance. *(F. R. Sherlock)*

made a second transatlantic voyage and on 21 June 1966 she left her home port for New York and a 38-day Fjords and Northern Capitals cruise, arriving back in New York on 7 August. Following this she carried out a series of shorter cruises from New York to the Caribbean and South America. This start to her career set the scene for her years with the Swedish-America Line with cruising making up most of her year, and occasional Atlantic crossings. On 27 December 1966 she sailed from Gothenburg for New York to begin a world cruise early in the year of 1967 by way of the Bahamas, Panama, Suva, Lyttleton and Wellington in New Zealand, then Melbourne and Sydney. From Australia she sailed north to Singapore, Hong Kong, Keelung, Kobe and Yokohama, before crossing the Pacific once again and returning to New York via Los Angeles, Acapulco, Panama and Port Everglades. Her first long cruise had been an unqualified success and, according to one passenger the ship had, '... behaved like the elegant lady she was, blessed with halcyon weather. And in one respect she was greatly fortunate; carrying 385 passengers, no one died and no one suffered any broken bones which, considering that the average age was 60 upwards, with a fair proportion in the active 80s, was nigh a miracle.'

Her next cruise, in the spring of 1967, took her back across the Atlantic, and in addition to French, Spanish and Dutch ports, she also called at Weymouth and Plymouth.

During the late 1960s and early 1970s the *Kungsholm*, like her namesake before her, continued her world cruise role with the occasional transatlantic crossing between Gothenburg and New York, which were more in the way of positioning voyages. Many of her cruises brought her to UK waters with calls at some very 'out-of-the-way' ports, as far as cruise ships are concerned, such as Llandudno, Avonmouth,

Torbay, Leith and the Tail of the Bank. In this way she just managed to remain profitable.

However, towards the end of 1973, with a depressed cruise market, steep increases in the price of oil and very high wage costs for the Swedish crews, the first signs of trouble appeared. Both the *Kungsholm* and the *Gripsholm*, which had been cruising from New York for a number of years, began to lose money. In an effort to cut costs, the Swedish-America Line attempted to transfer both ships to the Panamanian flag, but despite assurances from the company that wages and conditions would be maintained, it was obvious that the number of Swedish crew members would be cut drastically and the Swedish trade unions defeated the move.

During 1974 the company kept both ships at sea, but with losses mounting it was clear that hard decisions would have

The *Kungsholm* anchored in Bighi Bay, Grand Harbour, Malta in October 1968, during a six-week cruise from New York. *(Alex Duncan)*

to be made. Finally, in early 1975, whilst the *Kungsholm* was in Colombo during a round-the-world voyage from New York via both Cape Horn and the Cape of Good Hope, the Swedish-America Line announced that both ships would be sold and that, until buyers were found, their cruising programmes would be cut back. The company was facing a deficit of 20 million kronar, which was blamed on a 25% rise in manning costs, an inability to adjust cruise fares to offset the decline in the US dollar and increased oil prices.

Meanwhile the *Kungsholm* completed her world voyage at New York on 21 April 1975 and the following day she left on a month-long cruise to European waters. At the end of June that year she left New York for her final cruise with the Swedish-America Line, a six-week voyage to the Northern Capitals. She made her final call to her home port of Gothenburg on 15 July and she anchored in Dublin Bay on 5 August, arriving back in New York on 12 August where she was laid up.

However, her career was far from over and that summer it was announced that she had been sold to Flagship Cruises of Bermuda, owned by Oivind Lorentzen of Norway, who intended to continue operating her on cruises out of New York. Although her registry was to be changed from Swedish to Liberian, it was announced that she would keep her name. As a condition of the sale it was agreed that the vessel would receive a thorough overhaul and so, on 11 September 1975, she left New York, this time with no passengers on board, and crossed the Atlantic for UK waters. Seven days later she arrived in the River Tyne where she went to Swan Hunter's shipyard.

The *Kungsholm* was officially handed over to her new owners on 6 October 1975 and, although the refit was completed at the end of that month, she remained laid up in the Tyne as her cruise programme was not due to start until 19 December. At the end of November 1975 her new crew arrived in Newcastle to join the ship and five days later she left for New York, this time flying the Liberian 'flag of conve-

nience'. As scheduled, the *Kungsholm* started her new cruise programme six days before Christmas and, as in her Swedish-America days, she was seen in many ports of the world. In particular, when she visited UK waters she regularly called at various British seaside resorts where her mainly US passengers could disembark to visit local places of interest.

For two years the *Kungsholm* continued to cruise from New York without any serious incident until early 1978. She had left New York on 5 January with 500 passengers on board, bound for a world cruise, and the following day she called at Hampton, Virginia, leaving Hampton Roads that evening. Eight days later, at 5.30pm on Saturday 14 January 1978, as she was leaving the port of Fort de France on the island of Martinique she ran aground and, despite the efforts of engineers, she was unable to free herself. The incident happened just after the pilot had left and the ship was half a mile from the shore, grounded on the Madrepore Bank. Local tugs came to her aid but could not move her either. However, as there was no danger to the ship, the passengers remained on board and full services continued to be provided. It was five days before one US and two Dutch tugs were able to free her, at 10.45am on 19 January, but, with a number of cooling-water inlets blocked, she was unable to move under her own power and had to be towed to Port Everglades, where she arrived on 23 January. Fortunately there was no serious damage and she was soon able to resume her world cruise, passing through the Panama Canal on 27 January, two weeks behind schedule. The cruise took her via Far Eastern ports to Hong Kong, Bangkok and Singapore, before sailing through Suez and via Alexandria and Gibraltar back to New York, where she arrived in mid-April 1978. As the passengers disembarked from their three-month cruise none of them knew that her owners, Oivind Lorentzen, had started negotiations to sell the *Kungsholm* - this time to P&O.

The *Kungsholm* flying the Liberian flag following her sale in 1975 to Flagship Cruises of Bermuda. She is seen here at Kiel in Germany during 1976.
(J. K. Byass)

P&O's Princess

After her purchase by P&O in the autumn of 1978, the *Kungsholm* was renamed *Sea Princess*. Following a three-month refit she took on a very different appearance, mainly by the removal of her forward funnel and mainmast, and the heightening of the remaining funnel. This view, taken on 14 January 1979, shows the ship shortly before she left the Bremer Vulkan shipyard on completion of her multi-million pound refit. *(R. Witthohn)*

In the spring of 1978 P&O were considering the future of their 24-year-old passenger vessel *Arcadia,* which had been built for the company's mail service to Australia. Since the early 1970s she had been used exclusively for cruising, but as she had been designed to carry both passengers and cargo, her upper decks were cluttered with hatches, king-posts and all the associated machinery required for handling cargo which meant she was outdated as a cruise ship.

However, the announcement in June 1978 that P&O had purchased the *Kungsholm* from her Bermuda-based, Norwegian owners came as a surprise to the shipping world. It was also announced that P&O Cruises would take delivery of their new ship in September that year and, after undergoing an extensive refit, she would be renamed *Sea Princess* and would replace the *Arcadia* in the Australian cruise market the following February. Mr Harry Spanton, the Chairman of P&O Cruises, gave the public some idea of what the company had in mind for the *Kungsholm* when he said, '... the ship bears a resemblance to P&O Cruises' flagship *Canberra* - a likeness that will be heightened when the forward funnel is removed during the refit.' Many were horrified that this

lovely Scandinavian liner should be so disfigured, but this was balanced by the fact that P&O had rescued her from what had seemed a bleak future. P&O Cruises had returned substantially improved profits the previous year and Mr Spanton went on to say that, 'The vigorous revival of our cruising business over the last two years or so has brought with it the need and opportunity to consolidate our success. Certain areas of world shipping are under stress at the present time, but this acquisition demonstrates that there is good potential in specialized trades such as cruising - an activity in which we intend to remain market leaders.'

After the completion of the purchase the *Kungsholm* left New York for the last time in her original guise in early September 1978, bound for the Bremer Vulkan shipyard, Bremen, Germany, where her multi-million pound refit was to take place. Three months later in early January 1979, with the refit almost completed, the ship presented a very different appearance following the removal of the mainmast and forward funnel and the heightening of the remaining one. Although it did nothing to improve her appearance, it produced a profile similar to P&O's other 'Princess' ships which

The *Sea Princess* in the Bay of Biscay.   (K. McCart)

cruised from the West Coast of the USA. During the refit 86 new cabins were fitted, at the after end of the Verandah Deck, which increased her passenger capacity to 840 in 400 cabins, each with private facilities, air-conditioning, telephone and radio. On the Promenade Deck the Carousel Lounge was built where the Sports Room had been, and this serves by day as a lido bar for the new swimming-pool just aft of it, and at night is a centre for live entertainment. For the most part, however, internally the ship remained the same as she had been in her early days. The original works of art by Scandinavian artists and craftsmen remain untouched - the paintings, murals and sculptures, which had been selected with such care in the 1960s, remain today to remind passengers of her origins. The sophisticated décor remains a feature of her elegant lounges and bars.

The official renaming ceremony took place on 15 January 1979, when Mrs Jill Spanton, wife of the Chairman and Managing Director of P&O Cruises, unveiled a plaque which commemorates the change from *Kungsholm* to *Sea Princess,* and Captain Peter Love, her first P&O master, took command. Unfortunately, unusually severe weather conditions delayed the departure of the new P&O ship and it was on 22 January, six days behind schedule, that she left the River Weser bound for Singapore where she was to take over a 36-day cruise which the *Arcadia* had begun in Sydney on 29 January. The cruise had been advertised as a '36-day Eastern Adventure' with calls at Brisbane, Rabaul, Hong Kong and Singapore, where the 650 passengers had the opportunity to 'ring out the old and ring in the new' as they were transferred to the *Sea Princess* to continue their cruise. The transfer took place on 21 February, after which the *Arcadia* went on to shipbreakers in Taiwan while the *Sea Princess* took her place in the fleet.

Tremendous interest was shown in the new ship and bookings for her cruises were good. Soon after her arrival in Australian waters she was visited by the Governor-General of Australia, Sir Zelman Cowen, and in the following months she became a very familiar sight in the Pacific. However, in March 1981 P&O announced that, as part of a major redeployment of its cruise fleet, the *Sea Princess* would be switched to the UK cruise market, whilst the older and larger 42,000-ton *Oriana* would be based in Australia. The *Sea Princess* sailed from Sydney on her positioning voyage in early 1982 and she arrived in Southampton on 21 April, only 13 days after the *Canberra* had sailed to war in the South Atlantic. She then underwent a three-week overhaul, during which all her public rooms were refurbished and bow thrusters were fitted to aid her manoeuvring.

Her first cruise was due to start on 14 May, but as the campaign in the southern hemisphere gathered pace, everything

The *Sea Princess* leaves Southampton for a cruise in the summer of 1982.   (N. McCart)

became very uncertain. It was only 24 hours before she was due to sail that the Ministry of Defence decided that the *Sea Princess* would not be required for duties as a troop transport, and she was able to leave on schedule for a 14-day cruise to the Mediterranean.

That year she made 14 more cruises and one of these, which commenced on 16 July, took her back to New York for the first time since September 1978. At the latter end of 1982 she undertook a 90-day world cruise from Southampton by way of Panama, Sydney, Durban and Cape Town, arriving back in Southampton on 17 April 1983. During her summer season that year, whilst on an Atlantic Islands cruise, she was manoeuvring to go alongside the pier at St Michaels, Ponta Delgada, in the Azores when her starboard propeller was damaged as it hit a submerged object. Repairs were carried out on her return to Southampton, when the offending blades were cropped back.

That summer, a journalist writing about his experiences on one of the vessel's cruises wrote: '... it was the *Sea Princess* herself that made us feel a little like the viceroys of creation. In every port we sailed into she was always the cleanest, smartest ship, and usually the biggest. When we anchored out in a bay, we went ashore in a trim white launch like visiting nabobs. Each day at sea had the same easy predictable rhythm as we woke to a flat-calm ocean shimmering under a flawless sky. Hours drifted by with scarcely a sound except for the plop of a quoit on deck, the murmur of idle conversation and the gentle shudder of the ship's engines. For those of a more restless spirit, there were plenty of activities

The blades of *Sea Princess'* starboard propeller are cropped back after her mishap in the Azores during the summer of 1983.   *(K. McCart)*

on offer. Each day an intrepid band of keep-fit enthusiasts fought a losing battle against the effects of the apricot trifle. In some distant part of the ship, we were told, vigorous water-polo was being played. In yet more discreet locations, masonic meetings and a pursuit ambitiously billed as "Yoga for All" were taking place. Happily none of these activities

At the end of 1986 the *Sea Princess* underwent a £6.5 million refit, which included being given a white funnel with the Princess Cruises 'Sea Witch' motif. She then joined the Princess Cruises fleet on the US West Coast, and here she is seen in Alaskan Waters.   *(P&O)*

Still in the Princess Cruises livery, the *Sea Princess* is seen here in the South Seas. *(P&O)*

was aptly described as her home-coming cruise, displaying once again a buff-coloured funnel and the P&O logo on her forward superstructure. On her return to Southampton on 6 June 1991 the *Sea Princess* resumed her UK cruising programme in conjunction with the *Canberra,* with both ships making world cruises during the winter months.

These two now venerable old cruise ships have at least another full year together, but what will happen after that is not so certain. The future of P&O Cruises is assured well into the 21st century for, in January 1992, the company announced that an order had been placed for the building of a 67,000-ton cruise ship for the UK market, which is due to enter service in April 1995. The new vessel, which is being built at the Meyer Werft shipyard in Germany, is to be called *Oriana,* a name which conjures up memories of that 'Last Great Orient Liner' of 1960. The new ship, although not looking exactly like the *Canberra,* will have very much the same atmosphere, and the co-ordinating architect is Robert Tillberg, the man who was responsible for much of the *Kungsholm's* interior design. Thus, the new *Oriana* will be a natural successor to both the *Canberra* and the *Sea Princess.*

In June 1991 the *Sea Princess* was transferred to Southampton and to P&O Cruises and, once again, she wears the traditional P&O livery of white hull and buff funnel. Here she is seen arriving back in Southampton from Singapore on June 6 that year. *(W. Sartori)*

trespassed in any way on normal civilized life.'

At the end of 1986 there came another change for the ship when, after a £6.5 million refit in Malta, which included painting the funnel white with the 'Sea Witch' motif, she joined the Princess Cruises fleet on the West Coast of the USA, cruising in the Pacific Ocean and to the antipodes. It seemed that the UK cruising market had bade farewell to the *Sea Princess,* leaving the *Canberra* as the company's sole representative based at Southampton. Fortunately it was not to be so final, and after four years away, the *Sea Princess* left Singapore in the early hours of Monday 6 May 1991 for what

An excellent starboard side profile of the *Sea Princess* on a northern cruise. *(Alex Duncan)*

The *Sea Princess* berthed in Malta's Grand Harbour on 1 October 1992, during a 25-night Mediterranean cruise.

(Michael Cassar)

The *Sea Princess* berthed at Heraklion, Crete, on 25 May 1993.

(W. A. Cole)

Into the 21st century with P&O Cruises. An artist's impression of the new 67,000-ton *Oriana* which is due to enter service in April 1995.

(P&O)

Sea Princess arrives at New York for the first time following her conversion.   *(P&O)*

The *Sea Princess* in the Bay of Biscay   *(K. McCart)*

A magnificent aerial view of the *Canberra*.

Southampton gave the *Canberra* a tremendous welcome after her service in the South Atlantic. *(P&O)*

Principal Particulars

	SS Canberra	MV Sea Princess
Length Overall	249.50m	201.17m
Length BP	225.55m	173.73m
Breadth Moulded	31.09m	26.52m
Gross Tonnage	45,270	26,600
Max Cont Speed	27.5 knots	23 knots
Cruising Speed	21 knots	21 knots
Passengers:		
First Class	548	108
Tourist Class	1,690	642
One Class (As built)		450
One Class (Cruising)	1,641	714
Crew	960	430

Acknowledgements

Mr William A. Cole, Woodmancote, Cheltenham, Glos: Mr Andres Hernandez, Miami, Florida, USA: Mrs Lyn Palmer, P&O Public Relations, London: Mr Norman W. Pound, P&O Chief Engineer: Mr Don Smith, Selby, Yorks: Mr Kenneth Vard, Hove, Sussex: Mr Ralf Witthohn, Bremerhaven, Germany: Finally to my wife Freda, my daughters Caroline and Louise, and my brother Keith McCart.

Other Titles From FAN PUBLICATIONS:

Famous British Liners:

Vol 1	*SS Oriana* - The Last Great Orient Liner £6.95.
Vol 2	*SS Viceroy of India* - P&O's First Electric Cruise Liner £6.95
Vol 3	*Arcadia & Iberia* - P&O's Sisters For The 1950s £6.95

Write for further details to FAN PUBLICATIONS,
17 Wymans Lane, Cheltenham, Glos., GL51 9QA, England.

Copies of the cover photographs can be obtained from Mr D. Smith,
7 Chapel Court, Hambleton, Selby, North Yorkshire, Y08 9YF.